TRUST QUOTIENT

A FORCE MULTIPLIER YOU CANNOT IGNORE

Virender Kapoor

Chennai • Bangalore

CLEVER FOX PUBLISHING
Chennai, India

Published by CLEVER FOX PUBLISHING 2023
Copyright © Virender Kapoor 2023

All Rights Reserved.
ISBN: 978-93-56488-66-3

This book has been published with all reasonable efforts taken to make the material error-free after the consent of the author. No part of this book shall be used, reproduced in any manner whatsoever without written permission from the author, except in the case of brief quotations embodied in critical articles and reviews.

The Author of this book is solely responsible and liable for its content including but not limited to the views, representations, descriptions, statements, information, opinions and references ["Content"]. The Content of this book shall not constitute or be construed or deemed to reflect the opinion or expression of the Publisher or Editor. Neither the Publisher nor Editor endorse or approve the Content of this book or guarantee the reliability, accuracy or completeness of the Content published herein and do not make any representations or warranties of any kind, express or implied, including but not limited to the implied warranties of merchantability, fitness for a particular purpose. The Publisher and Editor shall not be liable whatsoever for any errors, omissions, whether such errors or omissions result from negligence, accident, or any other cause or claims for loss or damages of any kind, including without limitation, indirect or consequential loss or damage arising out of use, inability to use, or about the reliability, accuracy or sufficiency of the information contained in this book.

CONTENTS

Preface iv
Introduction x

CHAPTER 1. What is trust and why is it important? 1
CHAPTER 2. Building trust is not rocket science 7
CHAPTER 3. Taking it forward 19
CHAPTER 4. Humane side of trust 36
CHAPTER 5. Building Mass Trust 50
CHAPTER 6. The levels of Military trust 71
CHAPTER 7. Patience is the key to build trust-
step by step 91
CHAPTER 8. International relations and trust 103
CHAPTER 9. Media and trust 113
CHAPTER 10. Business Trust 126
CHAPTER 11. Political trust 142
CHAPTER 12. Building False trust 158
CHAPTER 13. People You Can Trust 167

Epilogue 174

PREFACE

TRUST QUOTIENT
A Force Multiplier You should not ignore

I have donned three hats as an adult and as a professional. I am a full time author now and have been writing books and articles for the last three decades. I was an educator, teacher and headed a top class B school for couple of decades nurturing, grooming and training young graduates running them through a two year full time MBA program. I also donned uniform and served the Army for good number of years.

This is where I am coming from and by education I am a telecom engineer, a post graduate in computer science from a prestigious IIT in Bombay and out of curiosity did a postgraduate course in strategic studies and International relations. This kind of a tap dance for decades on a chequerboard gave me opportunities of dealing with different situations, different people, bosses, colleagues, vendors, subordinates and students who are neither subordinates nor colleagues.

Preface

I worked with great people, real great leaders who taught me a lot and also with some nasty ones and that is how life pans out for each one of us. I had wonderful colleagues, wonderful subordinates. I faced difficult sometime life threatening situations. Overall a great learning experience.

At the end of it all I became a little wiser and could understand and interpret things in a matured manner. From technology I shifted my focus to human relations, human behavior and put all my energies to help people do better in personal and professional life.

Having written books on leadership, military ethos, military operations, bosses, Emotional Intelligence, Passion, work life balance, personality/biographically motivated books on human excellence I came a long way. I also wrote value education books for school children as young as six years!

All along my journey I worked on a principle of trusting people as far as one could. This was across the board. In most cases I was not let down as most of us humans are good and trustworthy- (that is what I believe). It cannot be all good all the time, but I took my chances and there were aberrations where trusting others ended in a bad experience but these were few and far between and I had to take it in my stride. This may not work for all and as we move forward to become a more civilized and more affluent society, the mutual trust has taken a hit.

I may not be totally wrong in saying that people trusted others more a hundred years back than they do today. Maybe there are more litigations, heartburns and even breakdown of families, relationships today than five decades ago.

Professionally it impacts every conceivable profession job or level of interaction- it is omni present

So in such a caustic- if I may say- environment, how do we work? Do we mistrust every one? Do people today back stab quickly and I have to keep looking over my shoulders negotiating office corridors and board meetings. How do I win trust of others as if everyone is on a mistrust spree, I can also become a victim of this imbroglio.

With so much of information flowing back and forth on internet through social media, radio and TV there are hidden agendas, personal propaganda, fake identities, frauds and fake news. It is difficult for us to discern wheat from the chaff in so much of information clutter.

In the entire scheme of things 'trust' becomes an important entity for a good work environment, dealing with people in general and also at home.

'Trust stress' is something which we get when we have to keep looking over our shoulders all the time. It is like getting a stiff neck, a frozen shoulder as you keep turning your neck all the time. You keep looking in your rear view mirror all the time which is stressful. It is painful to live like that. To top it all I feel everyone else is also looking at me from 'mistrust tainted glasses'!

In many places one is not sure of the intention of the person serving you. For example at petrol pump you need to keep alert that the guy is not filling less fuel and charging you more. You need to see that the bar tender is not short pouring a drink from the bottle or the medicine/food item you take is not past expiry date. Today 'shrink-flation' is a new idea which manufacturers have come up with, where instead of 100 gram potato chips they give just ten grams less and in almost a similar pack give you 90 grams charging for 100 and you will not even come to know. They are smart enough to print the right quantity as 90 grams but how many times we read this? You trust that all is well where as it is not. A million packets sold in a day is a huge saving for the company. In a way it is unethically ethical.

I just described the extreme southern side of the 'trust tip' but still there is humility and humanity left in big chunks in humankind and one can always look north and turn around things. There are still trustworthy people who have a right to mistrust others given the present condition of our society at large. We need to learn how to navigate through this mine field where you are always worried that the next step you take will land on a mine.

We need to establish a workable 'Trust Quotient' at work place as well as while dealing with others in general.

Remember- trust increase the speed at work, speed in getting things done. Therefore it has much more value than that of 'nice to have' a good mannered polite behavior-No- it is like oiling a rusted machine. It acts like a lubricant and make every machine move faster and faster is more efficient which brings the cost of operations down.

Meetings are time wasters and everybody plays meeting- meeting in corporate office- it is an organized way of wasting *Precious* time. Imagine the salary or cost to company of senior leadership- every hour is cost to the company in thousands of dollars and to your bottom line it is a killer.

Bottle neck is at the top of the bottle.

So if top management is locked up in meetings for half the day how much do you lose? Do a video recording of a top level meeting- you would see that half the time is wasted on disagreements, settling suspicions and squabbling on things which can be resolved in minutes if people have faith in others.

The other spin off is that top managers have their own teams waiting to meet them when they are locked up in a meeting, which further slows down the system! It has a domino's effect.

Imagine because of mistrusting a few (terrorists) a multibillion dollar security industry has sprung up- CCTV, scanners, security checks, long lines at security gate, of course it generates employment but at what cost? Time of the travelers goes down the drain. Everything crawls including traffic due to barricades and check posts every one mile.

'Honor among Thieves' is an old adage. Thieves will not steal from each other. In other words, this proverb says that criminals observe a moral code of honor in that they do not do anything illegal to their partners in crime.

Not a good example to go by, but even drug mafia or mobs or Sicilian mafia has 'unethical ethics'. They work on trust where millions exchange hands with ease.

That is why this book.

The content and approach

I would like to catch the bull by the horns and that is my style. I would utilize my experience donning all my three professional hats and create two outputs for the reader.

One how to make people trust you and two, how to handle, understand people and make them raise their trust quotient. The entire narrative will be built to achieve these two objectives.

– Virender Kapoor

INTRODUCTION

BUILDING CULTURE ON TRUST AND RESPECT THAT LASTS

"The thing that I have learned at IBM is that culture is everything."

– **L V Gestuer**
Former CEO IBM

How you differentiate a good organization from the bad? One word answer to this is "Culture." Work culture is that intangible ingredient of the organization which actually makes it tick. Top management and especially the leader of the organization has to make sure that setting the culture of the organization right is right on top of his priority list.

I would not like to go into the technical definition of culture but would put it in simple words. "Organizational culture is how an employee feels about the organization." Do employees feel happy, satisfied and motivated or they just come to work to draw their pay cheques? Organization is not brick and mortar, but it is the flesh and blood of the people who work there. You may feel very motivated and happy working in a small restaurant as a manager but may feel suffocated in a five star hotel as a lobby manager because of a bad work culture.

The first thing is that every employee should have trust in the organization that he or she works for. Leaders or powers that be must therefore build an environment of trust. In addition everyone should have some sort of a sense of security. This doesn't mean that people will get paid and retain their jobs whether they work or not. It means that if a person is doing his job sincerely he need not worry about his job or his promotions/remunerations. People must find that they are in a professional environment where you are paid for performance and not paid for invisibles like caste, creed, color or favoritisms. It should be a free space to work where everybody should be able to breathe freely.

Politics if played in an organization can really mess up the culture of an organization. You may do whatever you want for the welfare of your employees but if you play politics, all of it will go down the drain.

These as in my view comes under the best practices of a company. If people have faith in me then why do I need a suggestion box outside in the gallery? They should be able to walk up to me and project their problems and I as a leader should be able to give them some satisfactory answer. In none of the organizations which I worked for, I had to resort to a suggestion box!

Redressal of grievances must be quick and judicious. If there is a problem then fix it. Don't dilly dally it. I have a friend who works for an Indian company which is known for its ethical values. It doesn't pay the employees huge sums but pays them more than decent salaries right up to the top management. I asked this guy who is a CEO of one of the group companies as to why he was working in that company for the last thirty years-and when the pays were not so very great.

His reasons as a CEO were three "These people respect every employee; they give me freedom to work as I wish to and most importantly they never ask me to do any wrong or illegal transactions ever." I feel these are the pillars of good culture, respect, freedom and space to work and also an ethical way of working where employees are not pushed around to make murky deals or transactions within or outside the organization.

One very strong message from this statement is that a good culture stops or at least reduces attrition. If there is a great work culture people would not leave you easily.

> *"The only thing of real importance that leaders do is to create and manage culture. If you do not manage culture, it manages you."*
>
> **– Edgar Schein**
> *Professor MIT Sloan School of Management*

I was giving a talk at a forum and talking about culture I said that Tata was a company which had a very ethical way of working and provided a good environment for its people to work. People therefore didn't leave them easily .During the question answer session one gentleman got up and said "Sir, I retired from Tata last year after working for forty years. I pray to god that in my next birth also I should work for Tata's-you are so very right!" There was a big applause from the audience. This is the power of culture "People don't leave organizations they leave bad organizational culture!"

Certain organizations show a community bias and it goes against them .If you promote your own or creed you can't last in a global market which has a huge competition. You need to get good talent irrespective of what caste they belong to. America is a great nation because it pays for performance .They have progressed so well because they reward the good guys. You could be anyone; you will progress and make money as long as you are good.

A leader must ensure that everyone is treated fairly, no double standards, no favorites and no partiality. Actually, to practice all this doesn't require any efforts.

The flip side is true; having prejudice, differential treatment, having blue eyed boys can be so much of a hassle to handle. Then why do it?

What differentiates between a good and a bad educational institute? Here again culture is the main differentiator. It is more pronounced in case of management institutes. All of them have computer lab facility, a library, good faculty, a cafeteria, an auditorium but then why one is doing better than the other? Here also a good culture makes the difference.

My own experience tells me that it requires a lot of effort on the part of top leadership to set up a good culture in the organization. But once it is in place, it makes a great work environment to work for. It is easy to instill a good culture when the organization has just been established. To change culture of an organization which is in existence for decades is a very difficult task. This I feel is the greatest challenge for a leader who takes charge of a sick unit or not so healthy organization.

Introduction

Out here the brick and mortar is not rotting, but the people and their minds are rotting. To turn around a company one has to just turn around the culture and you will see spectacular positive changes very quickly. My advice to start ups is that establish a good culture from day one, it is much easier to do that. I have lectured at many places where I addressed principals and heads of educational institutes on "How do you make an educational institute vibrant and ticking." At the end of the lecture people come and tell me that they have been in the business of education for so very long but never realized these things which were so easy to implement.

A good vibrant organization ensures that people stick to it and you may well be surprised that attrition reduces to a large extent. It increases the overall efficiency of the organization and also makes people more effective .A good culture is like a pot of honey which will attract good employees to join you. As a leader your job is to make people proud of being a part of your team and a good culture does exactly that.

If one can start trusting people it will be great, because I am sure we have large number of good and honest people. Remember somewhere deep down everybody has a conscience. It is a matter of give and take and it surely works.

> *"The way management treats their associates is exactly how the associates will treat the customers."*
>
> **– Sam Walton,**
> *Fonder Walmart*

CHAPTER 1

WHAT IS TRUST AND WHY IS IT IMPORTANT?

You must trust and believe in people or life becomes impossible

— **Anton Chekhov**

*M*y experience of more than 40 years in various professions has taught me that the biggest dividend trust gives is- is a very comforting feeling!

What is trust?

Trust can be defined as "relying on the character, good will, ability, capability, support, of someone." This simply states that 'Trust means that you rely on someone else to do the right thing all the time'. You believe in the person's integrity and ability as well as strength, to the extent that you're able to take risk because of him or her.

Trust is essential to any environment or situation, because it provides a sense of safety and security. It is comforting. When your colleagues feel safe with each other, they feel at ease to open up and be themselves.

Have you dealt with people who don't trust one another, then you'll know how difficult, painful and draining this can be. Once there is no trust, people fight over small things and make a mountain out of a mole hill if they can. They create road blocks on purpose. As a result things slow down and environment is vitiated, polluted. People keep watching their backs. It doesn't matter how talented your people are, they may never reach their full potential if trust is lacking.

A slow organization becomes inefficient and pays an invisible *higher surcharge of trust deficit.*

When trust is in place, everyone is relaxed and becomes stronger, as he or she is part of a happy trusting organization. When people trust one another, the group can achieve truly meaningful goals.

Let me tell you a hilarious anecdote. There was a guy who walked into a bank and saw a handsome parrot with his friend. He asked if he would sell the parrot to him. He was told that this would cost him $ 2000 or 1.5 lac Indian Rupees. The buyer found this to be very expensive and asked what was so great about this parrot that he was asking for a ridiculously exorbitant price. His friend said that this parrot had special ability as he could fly with just one wing and was like a family and like a team member of the bank staff. This man was impressed and wanted to see this rare feat before clinching the deal.

So his friend proudly release the parrot into the air and lo and behold the parrot used only right wing to fly. Deal was done and having paid the amount he took the parrot and went away smiling.

Next day the chap came to return the parrot and asked his friend to return his money as he had cheated him. The parrot embarrassed him in front of his colleagues in his office. He said that in his office he got everyone together to see the special parrot fly on only one wing and as he released the bird, it let him down and was flying using both the wings. His friend again demonstrated the parrot's special capability and lo and behold the parrot was again flying only with right wing.

His friend was astonished and asked 'How come in my office it flies on both the wings and in this office it flies only on the right wing?'

His friend replied 'Because sir in this office everyone uses his left hand to cover his ass- and so does our parrot'

The moral of the story is that if in an organization there is no trust, it leads to suspicion and fear and people cover their behind lest someone stabs them in the back and they work on half their efficiency- single engine flying.

Mistrust and doubting someone is the biggest problem for us human beings. As we have become so very greedy and selfish that most of us feel that others are like us only!

We all have heard the 'Cry wolf 'story as kids where a boy in a village tending to his sheep raises a false alarm that a wolf had come and shouted for help. Villagers came in big numbers to help and found the boy giggling and teased the villagers. He thought he was just fooling around. Villagers were a bit annoyed but went back to their work. He repeated this a couple of times and fooled around each time, as the villagers came running every time. Once the wolf really came and the boy really yelled for his life and to save his sheep. This time villagers did not trust him and no one came to help and the wolf killed one of his sheep and the boy climbed a tree to save his life.

This is a simple story that has been repeated time and again to tell us that once people feel you are not telling the truth, they would never ever believe you and even in crisis will not turn up to help you.

In the month of August 2022 Elon Musk one of the richest business tycoon tweeted saying he was going to buy Manchester United, then quickly said he was just joking. Musk is currently the wealthiest person in the world with a net worth of $267 billion, according to the Bloomberg Billionaires Index.

"No, this is a long-running joke on Twitter. I'm not buying any sports teams," Musk replied, after his original tweet garnered nearly 500,000 "likes" in a matter of hours.

Such actions are detrimental to the reputation of a man who is the Tesla and SpaceX CEO would certainly lose his credibility amongst the general public.

Trust is to be built over a long period of time and as adults in positions of power or responsible professions cannot play pranks like these.

In the corporate parlance there is a role of a mentor who is a person who helps senior executives to navigate professional challenges. This relationship is semiformal and the mentor acts like a 'friend philosopher and a guide' for the mentee. This is a serious work and some ones job is at stake and mentor better be serious about his support and damn sure about what he advises. Mentor in a classical way is someone who is a 'Wise, trusted, counselor'. You may have wisdom and you may be good at counselling, that is a given. But are you trusted? A senior executive, a CXO level person or a CEO of a company needs to have complete faith in you, a hundred percent trust in judgement and confidentiality before he can take someone as his mentor. Trust in this case also is of paramount significance.

Let me make it clear, you just don't go and get a guy, most of the times a mentor could be a super senior in your industry who nurtures you, advises you and provides comfort during difficult and challenging times.

> *"To earn trust, money and power aren't enough; you have to show some concern for others. You can't buy trust in the supermarket."*
> **– His Holiness the Dalai Lama**

During my long experience I built trust for a personal motive- 'I wanted to be at peace and enjoy my work and deliver my best every time.'

I could do this in such a manner that it became a part of the culture and there after my organization would be on autopilot. I think this should be the ultimate aim of the leader or the head of the organization.

This works for every organization, be it a corporation, a manufacturing unit, a sports team, a hospital, a school or a college, an army unit, an air base, an aircraft carrier or whatever - trust is like one size fits all.

One size fits all is good to go as long as you do not use one singular template to achieve it. The way to achieve may be different, the syntax could be different but semantics and connotation remain the same.

> *Whoever is careless with the truth in small matters cannot be trusted with important matters.*
> **– Albert Einstein**

Questions for you

1. What are the three most important factors to build trust?
2. What lesson you draw from Parrot's story?
3. What is the biggest personal gain in working in an environment/work place where trust is palpable and visible?
4. How do you feel trust is shattered if one fools around with people? Give an example.
5. What do you understand by "To earn trust, money and power aren't enough; you have to show some concern for others. You can't buy trust in the supermarket." – His Holiness the Dalai Lama

CHAPTER 2

BUILDING TRUST IS NOT ROCKET SCIENCE

"Trust men and they will be true to you; treat them greatly and they will show themselves great."
– Ralph Waldo Emerson

Confidence building measures

I was fortunate to have worked in very different job environments. I served the armed forces where trust was a mandatory function without which you cannot move an inch- lives are at stake, tax payer's money is hugely invested, and the whole nation expects you to deliver as you are the last bastion of a nation's survival. Above all the honor of your flag and your nation is at stake. The stakes are unimaginably high. The boots on ground will never follow you in action or battle if they do not trust you. It is as simple as that. Those who have not faced this cannot understand the feeling you have in such situations and situations are ever evolving and things seldom go as planned.

Sometimes you need to act fast else the losses could be colossal. An incidence I would like to quote. I was posted in a Hilly area prone to landslides, cloud bursts and frequent flash floods. It is difficult for anyone to imagine the speed, ferocity and the sudden buildup of water volume in rivulets which causes flash floods. That is why these are called 'Flash floods'. One fateful night I get a call from my forward deployed platoon sized detachment that it had started pouring heavily and there was very little visibility. This detachment had weapons- small arms. They also had communication equipment and cold climate clothing. They were housed in make shift tin sheds on a little patch of a high ground along which a rivulet used to flow. Apparently one does a proper reconnaissance before putting up a semi-permanent tenement. All this done, you can still never predict how weather behaves in these areas and how it can impact these dwelling units. The buildup of water is so fast that you barely get minutes to save yourself. Within minutes I got another call from the Detachment Commander that he could see a tsunami building up approaching their camp. "What should we do sir?" was a panic stricken voice of the guy on the radio patched to my phone. I was more than two hundred Kilometers away and in no way help except take a quick call to save lives. There was no time to consult any one and I said 'leave everything and run up the hill all of you'. He shouted 'Sir what about our equipment?' I said 'just run and save your lives!' And the line went silent! Whoosh must have been. They did that and within minutes the entire camp was washed away but my boys were saved. Next day many down the stream from different units were not that lucky and several perished whose bodies were found miles down the river which was quite now.

This incident shook everyone but I was glad that we could salvage every man, yes the equipment was lost but lives are more important. This is a judgement call and no one can be perfect in such situations. But this act earned me respect, gratitude and built trust. Next time they would trust my judgement as now they felt they could count on me.

Just to let people know that when officers get commissioned in the Army, as young officers popularly called YO's are given a training in the units in a very unique way. Officers for first few weeks especially in infantry are made to stay with the troops and follow their routine. They stay with them, they eat with them, drink with them and run with them, doing all the obstacle courses and physical training alongside. They participate in Long range patrolling, firing practice and every possible activity. To dig along with your troops is a great bonding exercise.

This may not be done by every unit but ultimately officers do all physical fitness tests and participate in route marches and BPET- Battle Physical Efficiency Test. In Physical training officers lead from the front and demonstrate their skill in handling weapons as well as firing.

In the corporate culture they say that you should dirty your hands, go to the plant floor and smell the grease and oil – not coffee and beans- to be with the work force. This is very reassuring to the people in the plant and also the sales force. Good companies send their young executives to accompany their sales men on the trucks delivering goods even in the rural remote areas. These bumpy dusty rides give you a true feel of how life is for the people in field and also earns you respect and trust.

College life is entirely different but basics remain the same.

> *"Trust is the ability for everyone in an organization to confidently rely on (and predict) that others will do the right thing and make good on their promises."*
>
> **– Marie-Claire Ross**

Having served the army I shifted to another noble profession- academics.

I was picked up to head a prestigious B School and this was to be a great learning turf even in my second innings.

As I had learnt from my earlier mentors that initially you must just observe and observe and observe, I just did that. Don't take any action till you know every nook and corner of your new organization. Believe me this works.

I did just that and within the first few months I learnt that the things were not at all as per my expectations and standards that I was used to. The institute was partially head less for a while as the earlier incumbent was handling two institutes at a time till a fall guy like me was appointed to take charge. Fall guy I said? Not exactly, but I was a bit dejected and one day sat in my office thinking what to do? Was it glass half full, sort of situation- no may be less than quarter full. Academic institutes have another major peculiarity. Whether corporate or Army there you deal with employees who are already trained, hired and paid. Here the game is totally the opposite- Students pay you and come to learn! In the corporate you deal with vendors and buyers who supply raw material and buy your finished goods respectively. Here you are dealing with parents who have totally different expectations. They are not buying soap! They are buying a great life for their children. The other buyers are the industry who are popularly known as recruiters. They have high expectations from colleges otherwise thought to be a limp education system. My take is different on this. Had our education system been that bad then how come majority of top doctors and software Engineers/professionals in the west can be from India? Most western universities have professors and deans who did their education from the same system. Top CEOs in the US are from India- product of the same system. Don't blame the system blame those who run it? And Now I had to run it.

Your vendors in a college are knowledge workers, faculty, industry honchos and guest faculty.

The system I inherited appeared to be in a free fall. Directionless, demoralized and to some extent a dejected lot. There was very little hope amongst the students and the staff. Now I had to decide my course of action. The worst- in fact at that time seemed to be the best and easiest- was to quit and say sorry I can't do this, thanks for your offer and reposing faith in me and moved on.

The second was to look at it differently. I said to myself 'What if I assume that I was given to start this institute from a scratch? How would I do it?' So I told myself 'Assume as if the whole building had fallen and I get a clean slate and I need to build again brick by brick all over again starting from a scratch, how would that be? Great, I could make the blue print myself, design every piece the way I perceive it. This was a Eureka moment. I was lucky that my boss was very good from whom I learnt a lot. Dr. S.B Mujumdar is a gem of a person and he completely trusted me and gave me a free hand. Yes it can be done I thought. I remembered one of my professors in the Computer science department once telling us that instead of 'correcting and debugging' a botched up software program, it is better to rewrite and run it- it is lot less painful and you at the end say it is my program that is running now!' I just did that- I emptied the quarter filled glass and collected myself together to start ab initio.

The first thing was to build trust- People had to trust me to let me begin. Let me tell you dealing with MBA students is not every one's cup of tea.

I did it differently- involve everyone and lead them. There are student committees in professional colleges. The major ones are- placement committee, seminar committee and academics team. They were either doing very little or they were doing sweet nothing and pulling in different directions. I had to provide a direction and also a glue to make them work like one team. These committees were being handled by one faculty member each. A typical bureaucratic format all colleges follow. I had to break this first- an old tradition! I got those faculty members and told them my mission. I wanted to learn and learn hands on. Wanted to learn from the students and what better than getting involved with committees. So there was no protest or objection from the staff, else they would have mistrusted me for not trusting them. First trust hurdle passed, I took all the teams under me and their heads report to me.

I took a joint session of students only and added a few more teams, more empowerment to more students the better. A guy in a committee feels that he is being trusted and he gives his best- better than an ordinary- noncontributing student. I kept in mind- I was chewing more than anyone could bite- but I trusted my instincts and I knew I could slog and get things right. I had a batch of two hundred smart students 70% were engineers, 15% were with corporate experience. Which senior corporate honcho will have such a young, qualified energetic team? This thought was motivating for me.

I therefore told them first thing first- I trust you guys and I will depend on you to take this institution to loftier heights. 'Are you with me?' and they all said a resounding yes. How was the josh? Stupendous. They were suddenly very attentive and I could see a bright spark in their eyes. I feel Pereto principle of 80:20 works here too. In fact if you leverage trust it becomes 90:10. I just did that and threw in a caveat in this equation. I said if you behave like managers, I will behave like a CEO and if you behave like school kids I will be a tough school headmaster. So the stage was set and It was reassuring that we were on track more importantly on the same page. I enumerated the trust equation little differently- and it worked all the way.

Within a couple of years and hard work, sincerity and trust I came out as a satisfied CEO with 200 plus guys in my corporation. Trust turned a college into a corporate Inc.

I feel there is always a suspicion, a hide and seek feeling between the staff and students and that is a feeling of Omni present mistrust that is why there are strikes and protests in universities and colleges. If you are sincere trust is easy to build- I did that.

"The more you control, the less you will be trusted; the more you hand over control, the more trust you will earn." Jeff Jarvis, Journalist and Author

Within a month of taking over the reins, I was told by my deputy that the national seminar- a prestigious annual function- of the institute was round the corner. Since the time was very short, I wondered what I could do to contribute. He said 'just watch, these guys will be able to do it and as such nothing much you can do. All topics have been decided, speakers and guest speakers as well as chief guests have been invited- invitations already gone and accepted.' Again I had to trust my deputy, students and God.

The seminar went of very well. Being my first one I was almost a guest, just watching the proceedings. It is a full two day event and we get more than two dozen industry speakers, media coverage et al. It was a great learning for me. I could see the potential and commitment of my students. This was reassuring and now I could trust them even more. As they say' Taste of the pudding is in eating.'

I made a mental note of how we could better it next time. Having congratulated the seminar team I got into the daily routine of running the institute – learning something new every day- where there is never a dull moment.

You must bring something to the table basis your prior experience. One should do this intelligently and in consultation with others to make it work. You should not use the same template and that is where people go wrong. I was very open to learning and used to meet Directors of other Institutes under the same umbrella to clear any doubts or queries I had. Everyone was very cooperative. When students and my staff saw this they were sure that I was making sincere efforts to learn. This built trust and confidence further.

> *"If it's not written, it never happened. If it is written, it doesn't matter what happened."*
> **– Sercan Leylek**

I wanted an after event report to be prepared for the seminar and let the students decide what went as planned and where they had gone wrong and how things could be improved. Economics, operations, timing, effort and optimization could be the suggested parameters. One briefing and the committee gave a detailed report and suggestion and pit falls for the junior team to handle the next year event. Of course the report was not perfect but it was a very good effort giving this being a first attempt. Documentation and follow up action is very important. When your write, lots of things become clear to you- you do a post mortem on yourself-yourself.

This report was taken as the basis by the junior team and that being the base line I told them how could they take it to much more greater heights- least effort (economy of effort in military parlance), financially economical yet the best. I was astonished at the way second seminar was conducted- much more better in content, better coordinated and better level of speakers- this was trust in action.

Once this done, we started focusing on Placements, after all everyone wants a job and that too a good one. This is the trickiest part of heading a B School and tough nut to crack. Now it was time to win trust of the Industry aka recruiters.

Once again there was a joint meeting which was now a regular affair at least one meeting a day. Look at the commitment from both sides- me and the students. They felt they were running the show and I let them with a bit of monitoring as I was also learning and testing the waters.

I asked the seminar team- why we have these seminars. The answer was that these help in 'placements' as we get to show case our college to the Industry and it helps in networking! Fair enough.

I knew where they were coming from like all B schools (students) feel and do. I said 'what about learning from these seminars? So much effort, so much money spent and we are not generating any knowledge which is supposed to be our primary task as an institute of excellence.'

Students were in for a surprise and I said the academic team will now be a proper committee with expanded role and a larger cabinet. They would sit through the coming seminar and record/note down what each speaker said and create a document which will be published as a proceedings and these will go to the Industry. Now they understood the meaning of generating and leveraging on knowledge. The seminar team would thereafter make presentations to the entire batch on each topic so that the content sinks in.

This meant hard work and since intention was right they put in their best. It was not bullying them into work but involving them through trust built on proper communication. If your team trusts you, your students are prepared to work on a trust quotient you can surpass any great corporation in the world in terms of performance. Education has no tangible profit line per se but the intangible is the most tangible. Your reputation flies like wild fire good or bad, your stake holders are very well connected- that is the student community- you don't require advertisement as your students are the true trusted brand ambassadors if they trust you that you genuinely mean good for them. I started on a clean slate but could write something worthwhile on it as we all had good intention, integrity and faith in each other.

We produced 24 carat first class seminar proceedings year on year, better and better which students were proud of and why not- it was their effort, I was just a catalyst. I was trying to change the way all of us see things- from only placements to producing some form of Intellectual property to stand out different and also in turn earn the respect of Industry and trust of our recruiters. This is true delegation- trust based delegation. My student profile was the youngest around 21 years and eldest with work experience, around 28 years. I told them that 2nd Lt Arun Khetarpal was martyred at 21 years of age, destroyed several enemy tanks in the 1971 Indo Pakistan war for which he was awarded PVC (Param Vir Chakra) posthumously. If the nation could trust a young man like him, my team was no less. They were happy that I could compare every young boy or girl with such a great figure. I also told them that Arun Khetarpal was my dear friend during our training days.

Happy they trusted me- for a decade and beyond.

> *We're paying the highest tribute you can pay a man. We trust him to do right. It's that simple.*
>
> **– Harper Lee,**
> *To Kill a Mockingbird*

Questions for you

1. What do you understand by Confidence building measures?
2. What do you understand by the quote: - "If it's not written, it never happened. If it is written, it doesn't matter what happened."
3. What is the best way to build trust?
4. Have you ever made an effort to build trust with your friends- and how?
5. Do you think delegation builds trust? Illustrate with an example.

CHAPTER 3

TAKING IT FORWARD

Trust has to be the highest value in your company, and if it's not, something bad is going to happen to you.

– Marc Benioff

One more important aspect of trust is that you can't build trust once for all and then leave it at that- no you got to keep reinforcing it, all the time constantly. It is a situation like New York or Mumbai- cities who never sleep. Also it is like any big metro, the work on infrastructure is always in progress.

Nation building too is a continuous process. Governments and Leaders come and go but the nation building does not stop ever.

I had to be at it.

Secondly it has to continue and remain consistent behavior in action. You cannot and should never fake trust. People watch you all the time. You can't behave differently in different situations and with different people. You need to establish trust with everyone and that means everyone.

Trust is a 'Multiway Street', let me explain how.

In business you deal with clients, employees, vendors, bosses colleagues, banks, media, investors, shareholders.

In a college you deal with staff, teachers, guest faculty, vendors and suppliers too. The next blob is parents and students.

You cannot use the same yard stick and (stick or carrot) for students and staff even if they are on campus all the time and dealing with each other on hourly basis. This is the biggest challenge because in the corporate world, everyone is an employee and same rules apply to all, not in a college.

You got to win trust of all the different entities whose expectations are very different. The biggest concern of parents for instance is safety, especially of girls. Mobile phones are the biggest trust busters, you don't know where someone is calling from. Is he/she in the class or wasting time and money of their parents? This is a genuine concern. Most important to deal with parents is to respect their concern and be a part of their issues which worry them. Half the battle is won if you interact with them- most Directors/principals go wrong here- and I used to insist that parents must meet me at the time of admission. It did take away a lot of time but I feel that was my job. One on one meeting is very reassuring and often parents said 'Sir now we are so happy to leave our child in your custody'. This is a huge responsibility too. When you tell the parents that we have 100% attendance compulsory they are thrilled. Unless you are sick and have a doctor's prescription you got to be in the class. This is the biggest return on their investment. We have separate lady faculties handling a cluster of girls and that way it's a close watch- any one absent is immediately found out and action initiated according to SOP (Standard Operating Procedure).

This was another thing I initiated- making SOP's. But I also know that too many of these become a problem as if you make one hundred of these, be rest assured, nothing will be implemented. Therefore good judgement, discussions and deliberations help making it into a reasonable number- which cannot be fixed, depends on your style and also on the type of organization. I for one don't believe in too much paper work.

> *"Every responsibility you get make it a pocket of greatness"*
> **– Jim Collins**

SOPs apart, one has to act swiftly to respond to any situation. One day I was having dinner in a restaurant with some friends and got a call from my registrar late in the night around 11 PM that there was some problem projected from our new campus regarding students. He also told me that there was nothing alarming and things were under control. I told him, notwithstanding, the next day I wanted to visit the new campus and meet the students- which was a Sunday. We left on Sunday morning and as I reached I was told that Girl's hostel was almost a kilometer from the mess and this new campus was a 300 acre layout quite far from the town and could be unsafe for the girls at night to walk on that road. So I asked for the students to meet me right then and we walked along the road together and I could make out that at night this could pose a problem. I then told the girls that when they go for dinner, all of them in one hostel cluster should make a small group of at least five people, carry a torch and a whistle each and move as a group. Same for returning back. This way there can be no untoward incident. Walking alone in dark was an emphatic no. If you act, hold their hand and provide solutions, you avoid complains and earn trust.

I also started a buddy system where two students were made into a buddy pair. This way boys or girls kept a tab on each other's wellbeing. If someone was absent his or her buddy would know the details.

These small actions are a matter of common sense but give rich dividends and are appreciated.

Complaint box

I have a complaint against having a complaint box which is proudly put outside the library by colleges or in corridors of power in organizations. Why? If you trust us walk up to us and tell us what is wrong. Students could approach me or any staff member and project what troubled him/her. I used to encourage parents to find faults and give me feedback. It helps as you come to know what the problems are and it also builds trust.

I had an open office policy, in the beginning you will have lot of walk-ins from students and staff but once they know you are approachable there is no sweat.

One day in my initial months I saw an elderly couple walking restlessly in the corridor. I asked my registrar as to who were these people and what did they want? I was told they were waiting to meet me and were parents of a student on campus. I was taken aback and realized there was no waiting room! Any way I called them in and apologized for the inconvenience and parents were pleasantly shocked and surprised and the father of the student said 'Sir we could never meet the principal of our son when he was doing engineering! We are so grateful for your time.' Was I the Prime Minister of the country- surely not- then why make people wait?

The next action was to make a sitting room for visitors. I was told we do not have space. I said create space and it was created. Just two small sofa seats, a table with flower arrangement a small painting on the wall behind, a telephone on the side table (those days we didn't have Mobiles. A magazine or two and as parents come give them a cup of tea and biscuits. Is this damn rocket science? No. It is very easy. We did it and the feedback was quick to come. I had a parent visiting her ward. She had come all the way from Ambala to meet her son. When she was treated so well she insisted meeting me and came and told me she was so happy that her son was with us. She promised me that she would tell all her friends back home about this!

This is how small things matter.

> *Trust is built and maintained by many small actions over time.*
>
> **– Lolly Daskal**

Let me illustrate this with an example of Lt Gen Bhagat

Lieutenant General Premindra Singh Bhagat VC, PVSM was a recipient of the Victoria Cross, the highest and most prestigious award for gallantry in the face of the enemy that can be awarded to British and Commonwealth forces. The Victoria Cross was conferred on him for his actions in the Sudan theatre during the World War II.

In July 1974, he became Chairman of the Damodar Valley Corporation, a major electric utility company. During his short tenure, DVC increased its power production from 45 MW to 700 MW, and its morale and productivity improved greatly.

Power generation is not rocket science nor is it intricate brain surgery the organization lacked the right leadership. Lt Gen Prem Bhagat, proved this in 1974 in Calcutta as Chairman of the Damodar Valley Corporation (DVC).

All it needed was political will, which he got from then Minister of Power KC Pant who backed his decisions and a drive to improve power generation. Unfortunately, he died just 10 months into his term as chairman but by then power production in DVC had risen fifteen-fold. He used to say that DVC suffered from low morale, apathy, too much paperwork, and bureaucracy that literally tied it into knots and resulted in sheer neglect.

Recently, a book written by Major General VK Singh, titled 'Leadership in the Indian Army', describes some of the ways he went about it.

Singh writes, "With his characteristic vigor and no-nonsense approach, he (Prem) got the sluggish behemoth moving and soon the results were there for all to see. From 45 MW in August 1974, the production rose to 700 MW by October 1974, an increase of more than 15 times in just two months."

He goes on to describe that on Bhagat's very first visit to the office he wanted to be introduced to all the staff. One old man shook his hand and started crying. On being asked why he was crying, he said that in all his years in DVC, this was the first time he had met the chairman. Soon he was visiting not only the power plants but also the homes of the employees to see what they needed. This led to a visible improvement in the amenities and living conditions of the employees.

On a visit to a power plant he realized that the very low productivity was due to the lack of spare parts. The file containing the requisition had been shuttling between various departments for six months. Bhagat got hold of the file and wrote, "Sanctioned" and signed his name below. "Now get on with it," he said. He increased the financial powers of plant managers. At another plant, he found it unthinkable that replacements for generators would take six months to be shipped from Japan. He ordered that they should be flown across. The incredulous staff wondered at the cost. "Much less than the losses we are incurring due to a shortage of power," said Bhagat.

Just before the Puja holidays in West Bengal, he heard that union leaders usually strike for bonus. He declared an 8 per cent bonus several months before and baffled the union. With much of the red tape removed and better working conditions, the morale went up in DVC. He once told me that the buck really stops at the top. One should not blame employees when the system is bogged down by bureaucracy. Change comes only from the top.

I had mentioned earlier that army teaches us very good things and one can use these very effectively in other organizations, winning trust and goodwill of people.

Power has only one duty - to secure the social welfare of the People. Benjamin Disraeli

My next few steps

An organization can be judged by its toilettes! Yes this is true. How can you have stinking toilettes with broken taps and sinks? I will not accept it. So when I saw the condition of the toilettes for students, I hit the roof. I knew renovating toilettes is expensive but it had to be done. I called the contractors too an estimate to do it and sanctioned the amount from the existing funds which were enough. I told them I want the best toilets for my students and no compromise on the quality. I wanted full mirrors- end to end and good quality taps and replaced the sinks and pots with new stuff. Students were very happy. I was told by some naysayers in the staff that students are irresponsible and would damage these things. I said they are our students and not monkeys. Nothing will happen, and nothing happened. The admin committee was formed with clear cut roles- keep the toilettes squeaking clean and I don't want them smelly. Get them washed three times a day and it went very well.

Students normally have complaints with the food in the mess. They want to get a five star meal at the cost of a dhaba food. On top of it they feel the management is taking a kick back- which may happen in places. That is human nature.

OK, you do it yourself. I asked the students to get their vendor of choice. You decide the menu and see what best can be squeezed out of the supplier. They were happy that there was no interference from our side and also learnt that unless you pay the market fair price, you will not get a five star treat. Everything was sorted, everyone was happy. I told the admin committee- you are would be managers, learn how to make budgets and negotiate for the best deal, and it worked very well for every one and we didn't have to spend a minute on these often raised complains by the students. They really learnt that there are no free lunches. If you want chicken Biryani you jolly well pay for it!

The next step was to work on the library and we got a good architect and I told her one line management directive. I do not want this library to look like a library! She was unable to get my point. Then I explained 'All libraries look dingy and dusty to an extent depressing. I want library to look like a coffee shop but no coffee please. I wanted the book racks to be colorful, tables to be egg shaped and lots of color around. Let me assure you such things don't cost a bomb- in fact using orange color instead of brown or green costs the same. Creativity in fact cuts cost. More bang for the buck it is. We got real good paintings, where I got involved myself to select, and ensured the whole thing looked sophisticated and impressive. I got the new library inaugurated by national head of a consulting company, this did send positive signals to the industry. So this library got us trust of students and that of the industry too.

Now I wanted something radically different- in fact two things. First I wanted to make a mural out of telecom scrap. I spoke to the PGM Pune region Mr. RL Dube and requested for as much scrap of old telecom stuff he could give me. I sent few students and faculty to visit their junk yard and get all old telephones, broken exchange parts and much more. We had enough to create a 'telecom man' with the help of a mural artist. It was something unique and was kept right in the center of the library. Neighbors envy owners pride- just scrap. Something like tiger of make in India!

'Trust is the highest form of human motivation. It brings out the very best in people.' - Stephen Covey

The second thing I tried was an open library. I took a combined session of both the batches and pitched a very radical proposal. I asked them what if we have an open library where there will be no one to monitor or check who is taking which book. You can take four books at a time as per norm and we stick to it. No librarian, no chowkidar. You are the librarian and sentinels too.

I asked 'Can I trust you?' And now there was a resounding yes. We constituted a library committee an extension of academics committee and let it go.

I was told this would be a blunder- students will steal books. So I in my next session told them that if 100 books get stolen we will revert to old chowkidar culture. No trust motion against students for the library management. I told my staff that on an average a book costs Rs 250. If 100 books are stolen it will be a loss of Rs 25,000.

This would be the cost of trust building exercise. A six credit course on 'ethics and trust' would cost more than this but here the cost benefit would be enormous- We are training future managers and I wanted to do it. It threw up another surprise, we did a staff stock taking after six months and found more than two dozen extra books! Students had gifted some books buying these from their own pocket money- they had written their names on the book- 'donated to my college'. Oh my god I could never imagine this in my wildest of imagination- this is the power of faith, empowerment and trust. As they say one never stops learning.

Next it was turn to improve the assembly hall. This was a PG course and I wanted it to be like a convention hall whatever it means- but there was a need to do a major overhaul. Again I went back to the students and asked to get any architect they knew. Within a week few names came on my table and most of them were young and with just a few projects under their belt. But they were keen to do this project and were ready to do it in my budget which is usually little frugal in educational institutions. I saw their portfolio and met their clients and I was clear what I wanted and gave a go ahead. I trusted my judgement and instinct and it turned out to be a great outcome. It was something to showcase and all our guest speakers from the industry were very impressed. I was very keen on a good sound system and we managed that too.

> *'Self-trust is the first secret of success.'*
> **– Ralph Waldo Emerson**

Trust worked and that taught me how to trust new comers and motivate them, guide them and things work. We are talking of startup culture only now. If we don't trust our youth then who will- we should learn to experiment as leaders.

Another couple of things the army teaches you which is now part of our DNA is to be with your people and monitor things yourself at regular intervals from welfare point of view.

Checking quality of food and having a meal with your people is a good practice. Therefore once a week my registrar and I used to have a meal from the students mess. It gives you an idea of how things are going and also sends a trust message that we care.

If a student is unwell and is in a hospital, I ensured that either I or one of my staff members visited him/her at least once a week. The admin team was tasked to send one student every day and give me the feedback. Trust me this small gesture is very essential and earns the institute a good name.

All good things are done and should be done in good faith and not to score brownie points. If you do good things for the organization because you genuinely mean it, the rewards come back automatically.

To put the system in place I had started a system of weekly written progress/action report by every student committee. One should know what was being done by each committee and if they needed any help from me- the second point being more important. Once they have to log their work they do it more diligently.

My instructions to my staff were clear. I want every mail/letter to be replied within 24 hours. If not send an interim reply and keep me posted. This is the biggest problem I witness and observe in our industry- people just don't respond. We are grooming future managers and how can we be irresponsible? The land line phone had to be answered in three rings- that is training of the staff and reflects on your professionalism. This is the difference between a five star hotel and a not so good hotel. This is not difficult provided you ask for it from the top and give it adequate priority. This let me tell you is a small thing but has a very positive impact on the parents and the environment.

You cannot bully and create a system- you got to be a part of it, train people, guide them and then see the results- they will be very good.

> 'A man who trusts nobody is apt to be the kind of man nobody trusts.'
>
> **– Harold Macmillan**

I had noticed that the filing system was not efficient- in fact it was inefficient. So I sat in the back office for a week to understand the loop holes. We bifurcated letters according to major subjects and created four or five different colored files for each subject like finance, admin etc (covers, folders) for quicker identification, we redistributed the letters accordingly. I had laid out a response time of five minutes, which meant that if a letter was to be put up to me, it should not take more than five minutes- it finally came to three minutes and less- my staff did it so well that they surpassed the level I had set! They were proud to do it. In fact initially they thought five minutes response time was too ambitious but they surpassed it themselves. They thereafter trusted my orders, my judgement and my deadlines. It built trust and faith in the entire team.

When any one joined us as a staff member, teaching or non-teaching. During my interview I made it very clear that I do not want any back biting or politics- come upfront. You have a problem, I am approachable. This is very comforting. You trust me then I trust you but if you don't trust me then don't expect me to trust you-simple. I am for technology but if you want something to be done, pick up the intercom and speak- don't play mail-mail. In a compact organization sending a mail for every silly requirement is not required. It in a way makes people feel that they are not trusted. For a pen/pencil I should not fill requisition forms.

> *"Thoughtless reliance on technology is a liability,"*
> **– James C. Collin**

Respect and response works- you got to make it work

Whenever any faculty used to join I ensured that his/her office was set up properly. I inspected it myself. When you enter your new office, you have a proper table and chair, a cupboard, book rack, fresh and washed window curtains, lights and fans functional your desktop (we had those days) your official mail ID generated, intercom placed and working, with a directory, your visiting card printed! A flower vas with fresh flowers on the table, a pad, a folder and pen stand and two visitors chairs. I ensured that there was a decent painting put on the back wall. A welcome card signed by me. Does this cost too much? No- not at all.

Imagine you enter in your office and you find it spotlessly clean with all this, how will you feel?

Even if you are the junior most lecturer it has to be done the same way. See the return of trust and morale and respect on this investment. Every new incumbent used to be surprised and to an extent shocked at this treatment. I look at it as professionalism and mutual respect for people who work for you. They never got this treatment elsewhere. Some of them came in an emotional state to tell me this. See how a person feels when he is treated well. He trusts the organization basis its efficiency and caring attitude, he becomes a part of the system on day one. His or her attitude towards his work and others is impacted positively.

> *The right to be respected is won by respecting others.*
> **– Vasyl Sukhomlynsky**

I had the data base created for all present and past students. It included their blood group and information about NOK next of kin, address and phone number. It appears to be a frivolous unproductive exercise. But listen to this.

A terrible accident

True colors of an organization are seen when it is under pressure or more in a crisis.

I was in Delhi for some work and got a call from a company who was a regular recruiter for us. Their HR head had my number and was on the line and informed me that one of their employees had been killed in a road accident and he was our former student. He told me his name- oh god, he was my former student. They did not have the details of his NOK- parents, their address and were unable to inform them. He wanted to request me if I could help in this regard. I was of course saddened hearing this news. I told him I was away from my office in a different city but I will get it organized as soon as possible.

I gave a call back to my office and asked them to dig out the details from our data base and revert back quickly. I was sure of my systems and response time. Within minutes we got the details including the telephone number of the parent which was passed on to the HR head.

Our SOP was clear, you have to first ring up the number and check if it is the right number of the right person. Once confirmed then only pass that number on. Many times numbers change and you pass on the wrong number and the other guy is in circles as that number is of no use, it is just like a sham.

Though this was not the time to take credit, yet I was glad that the HR head had the decency of calling me back and appreciating my efforts and our efficiency. I was surprised that professional organizations in business do not have records of their employees and have to look elsewhere to get information. I was satisfied that my staff and system could respond to any emergency. But this should be a lesson for the corporate world and all organizations to keep data of each and every employee and keep updating it regularly.

> *"The good-to-great leaders never wanted to become larger-than-life heroes. They never aspired to be put on a pedestal or become unreachable icons. They were seemingly ordinary people quietly producing extraordinary results."*
>
> **– Jim Collins**

Questions for you

1. Can you build trust once for all and then move on? Explain with example.
2. Explain how trust is a multi-street affair.
3. What do you understand by 'Trust is the highest form of human motivation, It brings out the very best in people.'
4. How did General Bhagat win trust in a short period? List 3 points.
5. Does training your staff and making them more efficient help build trust? Explain in your words how?
6. How do you think respecting others builds trust?

CHAPTER 4

HUMANE SIDE OF TRUST

"There are many things in life that will catch your eye, but only a few will catch your heart. Pursue those."

— **Michael Nolan**

It is emotional to a large extent

Whichever way one may like to look at it, one thing is certain that human nature, response, reaction and human nuances in general play out loud when we talk of trust. Simply put it is an emotion. It is touching and reaching out other hearts through your heart and not via your head. Striking an emotional chord with others is at the center of it. It is much harder to understand human behavior than number crunching.

Let me begin by giving an example. How does a girl trust a boy or a woman trusts a man and is ready to be escorted alone by him in the dead of the night to be dropped at home? There is no way, no one formula to win trust of a lady. It is done over a period of time or could never be achieved over months or wooing for years. Nobody has ever been able to solve this puzzle over the centuries.

As Blaise Pascal says "The heart has reasons that reason cannot know."

Taking a cue from this I would say 'It is like good or bad vibes when you look at trust. It's a heady mix of body language, facial expressions, and your tone and behavior.' Behavior is your action and reaction to every situation which people watch very closely. A child also understands whom to trust and whom not to, he knows who will harm him and who will protect him.

One way vibes could be defined as 'a person's emotional state or the atmosphere of a place as communicated to and felt by others.' And fits into the scheme of things as we go forward. Radiate kindness like confetti.

The more you put your heart into things, the better it feels when something yields results.

Closest to trust in texture comes 'charisma'. Like many human traits and qualities, charisma is not something you simply have or don't have. There are different ways of defining what counts as charisma, and some people possess certain—or sometimes, many—charismatic qualities in above-average proportions, from a talent for emotional storytelling to beaming confidence.

Charisma also impacts people at emotional level when one could be spell bound in some one's presence. A charismatic personality is someone who displays both social and leadership skills. They have warmth and competence that engages and persuades others. These behavioral traits can be learned, such as self-awareness, open body language, active listening, and treating each person you encounter with equal respect. Charisma begets trust, faith and confidence.

Winning trust of animals

This may sound trivial and irrelevant but it is not. In fact Animals do have a very peculiar sense of judgement. They can make out the present and clear danger faster than humans.

> *"If you pick up a starving dog and make him prosperous he will not bite you. This is the principal difference between a dog and man."*
>
> **– Mark Twain**

Dogs know who is a dog lover and would straight come close to you wagging their tail without any hesitation- pets or street dogs- they sense trust. They can recognize you after years of separation.

Horses too can sense trust. If you are a good rider they can make out as soon as you sit on the saddle. They also understand who is scared and who is not.

Horses are very feeling-oriented animals. Their survival depends on an innate ability to sense their environment. They watch and react to everything – as well as communicate with the herd – depending on their surroundings. If one member of the herd gets scared, the entire group responds together and seeks a safer environment.

Therefore try to keep your emotions in check while dealing with horses if you want to win their trust. In doing so, you essentially become a member of his herd by communicating and helping to keep him safe and secure.

Of course it is a lot difficult or may be not possible to win trust of predators and wild animals- they are unpredictable and can attack if they sense any threat.

> *"If there are no dogs in Heaven, then when I die I want to go where they went."*
> **– Will Rogers**

Let me illustrate the humane side of trust with some incidents that I personally encountered.

A lady in distress

As a head of a management Institute I had a number of women as faculty and non-teaching staff. One day a lady who used to be a good teacher came to my office and wanted to discuss something personal. She had two growing up kids and was not getting time to help them with their studies. She was worried as they were now in senior classes in school. I wanted to know exactly what was going in her mind. She said that she wanted to quit the job so that she could spend time with her children and help them with their studies.

I could have asked her to put up her resignation and let her go. But I instead wanted to do something that would be something like 'Have the cake and eat it too' situation for her. So I immediately told her that after a few years when her kids go to college, what would she do? She had no clear answer and it was my job to advise her correctly. I told her that probably then she would regret her decision. I wanted to give her a better option.

So I asked her what if she comes for half a day and work on half salary? This adjunct faculty status was good for the college too- I would retain my talented faculty and she could finish her teaching contact hours in the same way. If you are willing to help someone there is always a way. She was so thrilled because she never expected this coming from me. Deal was done and I told her to register for her PhD too. She did that and could look after her duties at home, teach in the college and she earned a PhD as well. We are still in touch and I am happy this worked for her. This was done out of a good humane gesture but this good faith percolates down the rank and file and builds tremendous confidence and trust in an organization. And let me add that she in those adjunct days did a wonderful job basis trust between the two of us.

To hell and back

Two of my good faculties got a better job with more salary and wanted to quit. Since there was no way to retain them and in their interest I accepted their resignations, had a farewell party and wished them luck.

After quitting they would have settled in their new organization. And that was fair to assume. But after a couple of months I got a call from one of them and he told me that he was not at all happy as the organization culture of their new outfit was bad and no one trusted the other guy and atmosphere was toxic. He said that the other guy who left also had the same feeling. He sounded very low and dejected. Since he trusted me and could confide in me he had called me and must have expected some response. So when I asked him as to what did he want from me he said that both of them wanted to come back and work with me - rejoin? These two had worked with me for several years and they had an exemplary record. I gave them my approval and asked them to join back. This was again a good gesture- which many may not have done- Bosses may hold this against those who quit- but this was also an exercise that built trust and mutual respect.

I cannot do this

Another incidence happened with one of my computer system manager. He had just joined and was getting married in a couple of months. He obviously wanted his earned leave. He wanted to go for one month that would be sufficient for wedding as well as honey moon. As his leave application came to me, there was a remark by my deputy director that since he was still on the six month mandatory probation period, he will have to go for his wedding without pay! In addition he told me (which I was aware of) that you earn leave after working for one full year, and he had done only two months till now.

I called my deputy to discuss this and he said no way we could pay him his salary for next month. I said that this rule was made to ensure that he doesn't quit and run away with his salary and he earns leave after he works for one year. 'What is his salary'? When he told me the amount. 'What if I take personal guarantee?' I said.

I said had it been any other reason for leave I would have sent him on leave without pay but will it be fair to ask him to go for his marriage without pay? Normally you give a contributory wedding gift to an employee for his wedding and here you want me to cut his pay? Not done. I said leave sanctioned and if he does not return I will pay his salary from my personal bank account into the Official account of the college. Bend rules to people's advantage- use discretion

How much trust you build with small gestures cannot be imagined. I knew he would come back and he did.

A mistake that was not deliberate

Mistakes do happen. No one is perfect- as long as it is not deliberately committed. One day a visiting faculty who was a very good teacher came to me and she looked distressed. She was very upset. She said 'Sir I do not know how to explain but I committed a terrible mistake' I asked her to let me know what happened. She said that she had her PPT for a class lecture on her pen drive and she had given it to a student to load it on the system in the class room, he down loaded the entire content which also had the final question paper on it! She wanted to apologize and resign and was almost in tears.

It was a mistake but she didn't do it on purpose, I found that it was not her fault, yes she should have been careful and not kept the final paper on the same device as her class presentation. The worst was that paper had leaked before the exam. I had full faith in her and discussed this internally to find an appropriate solution.

We had to do a retest and take necessary actions to reverse the damage done. This was a lesson learnt by her and also propagated to the rest of the concerned staff. This built trust between the system and the stake holders.

You learn from well-meaning people

Mr. RL Dube was the Principal General Manager (PGM) BSNL Pune circle, a very senior officer looking after the entire area of the city and also some adjoining rural areas. A busy man with lot of operational day to day responsibilities. I had the opportunity to interact with him several times either in my college or in his office. One day while having a cup of tea with him in his office I noticed that he was taking calls from subscribers who had complains about their telephone lines. Those days the most important mode was a land line as mobiles had yet not hit the Indian market.

He was talking to the agitated subscribers very politely and assured them that their telephone will be repaired at the earliest. Imagine he was doing what an operator to handle subscriber complains was supposed to do. He would take at least five such complaints in a day and would pass on the problem to be actioned to the General Managers of the concerned area. He would ask them to give him a feedback once the fault was rectified. I was very surprised that why such a senior officer would do it and asked him about this. He said 'I look at it this way, if a customer is giving me a call he must have got fed up of the system. Unless he was exasperated he/she will not ring me up. First it lets me know that all is not well and we need to pull up our socks. Second it gives the complainant a satisfaction of immense order and he trusts the system, after all if I spare one hour a day, the positive impact and trust building is more than my time invested. I wish our public servants learn from this and obviously Mr. Dube was a respected man in the department and held in great esteem by the subscribers.

He also narrated an incidence regarding application form that has to be filled by a subscriber requesting for a telephone. Before the (NTP) National Telecom policy got implemented and much before the mobile revolution and privatization invaded us there was a long waiting to get a land line. The forms were sold at a counter on the ground floor of the building where PGM Mr. Dube's office was. He said for one week he stood at the counter where the forms were being distributed. He said one day a person applying for a telephone came to me with the huge form and said 'Sir can you see how difficult it is to fill this form? You are asking for so many details from us which may be of no use to you at all. You are giving just a telephone for which I am paying, I don't understand why you cannot simplify it?'

Mr. Dube was embarrassed but he said he appreciated the point and brought one copy of that lengthy application form to his office and started filling it himself! He told me that he himself found it so difficult and with so much unnecessary information to be asked from a customer. He said he called a meeting and asked concerned officers to make it very simple- just ask the essentials and nothing more. In a few weeks a new form was being distributed- this is how your customers respect you and you build a rapport and trust at grass root level.

Some more learnings about respect and trust

I have a friend who was a very senior professional with the Tata group and worked very closely with Mr. Ratan Tata the chairman of the group. He told me an incidence which is worth mentioning. He said he had a meeting with the chairman in his office and at the end of it he reminded Mr. Tata about an award ceremony. He asked Mr. Tata if he would be coming for the award ceremony for employees of Tata group in a company located somewhere in East Asian country. It was an award which was chairman's award and he was always present to hand over the awards to the senior members himself. This was a custom followed all the time. Mr. Tata told my friend, yes I will try to come. This surprised him but he never asked him to confirm and moved on. He says that Ratan Tata came for that function all the way from Mumbai and as he was getting down from his private plane, he had his entire one leg bandaged and he was walking with a stick, slightly limping, but still carried his own brief case. He smiled and told my friend 'I told you I will try to come because I was to undergo a surgery which was scheduled close to the dates of award ceremony and I was not sure if my doctor would permit me.'

To top it all he refused to sit and give the awards and stood for almost an hour to hand over each award and shook hands with each man and woman recipient. My friend could make out he was in pain but he did this to win confidence of the team and also earn respect and forge trust.

An incident mentioned again by a very senior employee, Arun Maira, of the Tata Group is worth narrating in brief. He says (input given to Mint) that in 1970, Tata set up their first production facility in Malaysia. The business didn't do well and the bank gave them a notice to wind up as the loans could not be paid. A senior banker came to their Mumbai office to deliver the ultimatum. All Tata Motors could do was to give a one-page letter of assurance signed by the CEO that they would do their best to repay the loan and would make all efforts to boost the business.

The banker wondered what that piece of paper and its assurance was worth. So he asked Deutsche Bank in Germany, who had been bankers to the Telco joint venture with Daimler Benz. The bank told him that a letter signed on the Tata letterhead by the CEO of a Tata company was better than the financial guarantee of a bank! And everything got sorted out. This is the power of trust.

I once had a problem with a very senior person in Tata Communication and a meeting for which I had traveled to Delhi was cancelled without me being informed. The worst was that no one bothered to redress my agony. I was upset and decided to write a letter to Mr. Ratan Tata narrating the incidence. Within a few days, I got a response from his office regretting the incident and promising to take corrective action! This earned the entire group tremendous respect in my eyes.

Deal done on trust- 'Zubaan'

When you make a promise or a commitment you must keep it. They say 'Word of honor' or 'I give you my word'. If you keep it people will trust you as it reflects a very sound, honest, committed character.

I remember I had a boss who was very humane, he was a hard task master but when it came to your wellbeing he was genuinely concerned which reflected on many occasions as I worked in his team.

He kept the same stance even after he retired. I remember he had built a Bungalow near Indore and had decided to live a retired life there. Sometimes things don't work out as planned and one has to take a different route. Something like this happened in his case and he decided to sell his house. There were a few buyers and he struck the deal with a person who offered him the best price. It was a verbal commitment with a very insignificant token amount exchanging hands. There was no paper work at all, not even a plain paper letter between the two.

After two weeks another guy came and made an offer of almost one a half times! My boss could have returned the token money and gone for a better deal.

He didn't give it a second thought and said 'Sorry I have already sold the house and given my word, I cannot go back on my word.' Bingo- I was so impressed by this act that it has made a lasting impression on me. Here I learnt what trust is in action.

> *"Trust is built when someone is vulnerable and not taken advantage of."*
>
> **– Bob Vanourek,**
> *Author of Triple Crown Leadership*

This stayed with me too and some others who worked with him. A friend of mine had a small piece of land which he sold and took the money from the buyer. Six months later the buyer who was a lower middle class individual came to his house and told him that for the land transfer he would have to sign some papers which he had not got signed. By this time the land rate had doubled. He could have refused to sign and returned the money for more profits but he did not do that- a word of a gentleman is to be honored. In today's world this looks foolish but there are several good people who still do it. Sometimes I wonder how much business lawyers would lose if people behaved this way- many lawyers will go out of business I am sure.

But one thing must be kept in mind 'Do not trust blindly'.

> *"It takes 20 years to build a reputation and five minutes to ruin it."*
>
> **– Warren Buffett**

Questions for you

1. Have you ever witnessed a transaction being done basis trust? If yes, can you recall it and write in a few words.
2. Can you say with conviction that trust is based on emotions and not logical reasoning?
3. Do people trust you most of the times?
4. Do you make efforts to build trust around you?
5. Do you trust others easily?
6. Have you ever been taken for a ride for trusting some one? If yes, write down the incidence.
7. Have you ever broken a major promise made to someone? If yes or no how do feel about it today.

8. Why Tata as a brand respected and trusted by people at large?
9. Name five people and five brands you trust. And why?
10. Have you put yourself at financial risk to help someone and built trust?

CHAPTER 5

BUILDING MASS TRUST

"Top 15 Things Money Can't Buy

"Time. Happiness. Inner Peace. Integrity. Love. Character. Manners. Health. Respect. Morals. Trust. Patience. Class. Common sense. Dignity."

– Roy T. Bennett,
'The Light in the Heart'

Every job requires integrity and trust as the fundamentals basis which client relationship is established and sustained. You need to trust even a peon in the office or an errand boy or a janitor before you hire him. Help at hand or a domestic maid at home is to be trusted before she is hired. A driver, a nanny, a plumber a security guard or an electrician has to be trust worthy to be employed by someone.

Cab services like Ola or Uber fail when their drivers are not trust worthy. Here he/she has to be on time, his car has to be reliable and the customer must be safe with such a driver.

When you go up the ladder, trust factor becomes more critical.

For instance consider the following professions.

1. Dentist
2. Surgeon/doctor
3. Pilot
4. Architect
5. Attorney representing your case
6. Police man
7. Psychiatrist/ counsellor
8. Auditors/Chartered accountants
9. Manager of a garage
10. Maintenance Engineer
11. Nurse
12. Judges/magistrates
13. Banker, teller, cashier
14. Investment consultant
15. Preschool teacher
16. Broker
17. Salesman
18. Veterinarian
19. Dog trainer
20. Life Coach/mentor

All the above require a trusted person whom you can confide in and who can be fully trusted for professional competence and reliability. Their services impact you so much personally that you cannot have even an iota of doubt in any respect.

Would you take your pet to a vet who does not know how to handle your pet and cannot administer an injection with ease and confidence? Will you go for a toothache to a dentist you don't trust? You will never allow to be operated by a surgeon whom you do not trust. You will never give your car for servicing where you have little trust.

In fact today trust has become more important as the entire economy is service based- at least a large component.

There are several related qualities to trust that must be clearly understood and accepted

Here I give a related cluster of qualities that go into building trust and also some of them are equivalent to the quality of trust.

> *"Brand is just a perception, and perception will match reality over time."*
>
> **– Elon Musk**

These are:-

Confidence, assurance, faith, acceptance, hope, belief, certainty, expectation, anticipation, dependability, security, safety, reliability assurance, promise, guarantee, credence, conviction, credibility, principled, positivity, conviction, even certitude.

Whenever you need to gauge trust, these could be useful as benchmarking tools, parameters to base your judgement on.

Alternately if you are into any of such professions- though trust is important in every job- you must take care that you base your reputation and trust on all these above parameters. I call it Mass trust because you are dealing with hundreds of different people who will come to you only if they trust you.

Integrated trust factor

In case you want to get your health checkup done, one major test is the blood test and you engage a Pathological lab for this. You have several in your town but basis feedback from friends and your 'trusted' doctor you repose your trust on say XYZ lab. You call them up and fix a time for their blood sample collection person to come home and take your blood sample. 'Trust gauging clock' starts ticking here after in your head.

First thing that builds trust is that he (person who has to take blood sample) comes dot on time. Then next you see that he has a neat kit and his needle and syringe is up to the mark. Third is how good he is in taking the blood sample- can he do it in one attempt, or he pierces multiple times to find a vein and hurts or he just takes it in one shot without hurting you. Now how he speaks to you confidently, smiles and moves out promising that report would be in your mailbox by so and so time. And you get the report in your mailbox five minutes before time. When you take the report to your doctor he is convinced that the lab had done a good job.

The key people involved in the process are

1. The person who booked your appointment on phone
2. The person who came to take blood sample
3. The lab technicians who performed the tests
4. The Pathologist who signed the report.
5. The person who uploaded the report and mailed it to you.

This entire team works to ensure that a customer is satisfied. This is what I call as 'integrated trust'. As the head of an organization big or small, this must be conveyed to each member performing a task.

> *"A brand for a company is like a reputation for a person. You earn reputation by trying to do hard things well."*
>
> **– Jeff Bezos**

Building a trusted brand- a perception

Tata is a brand one can trust blindly in a way. Similarly cars like Mercedes, BMW have created their name over almost a century. It is very difficult to take them down- it is a solid trust, a reputation of their name.

Among Indian brands Tata comes out as number one. As a test I do a small exercise with every incoming MBA batch. In a normal conversation on motivation and leadership, I ask a question rather casually 'How many of you trust TATA as a brand?' without hesitation you see all hands going up! This happens year on year every year.

Tatas have been working consistently, not to build a brand but to build respect- that is the difference. Advertisement can inform people about you but cannot get you respect and that is the basic difference- your work, consistency builds reputation, respect and then trust.

Dubai and in fact the entire UAE has built not only great infrastructure but their rulers have created so much of trust that overall UAE is a trusted brand. Why so many westerners settle down in UAE and feel safe there more than any other Arab country? There are 22 Arab countries and because of transparency and being trustworthy they have prospered more than any other Arab nations.

The citizens are told- the Arab nationals that you will treat everyone with utmost respect and you can see it, you can feel it.

I was in Dubai to deliver a talk basis one of my books almost 15 years back. One of my suitcases was full of my books and was therefore very heavy. At the customs during scanning electronically the customs officer asked me what was I carrying in that baggage. I told him that these were my books and I am an author. He asked me to take it down and open it for inspection. I did that and he found only books and smiled 'Oh you are an author, good to meet you sir!' I gifted him a copy and told him that I have a back problem and I cannot lift this heavy suitcase. Promptly he called a porter, loaded it on my trolley and came to see me off till my car waiting to take me to my hotel. This is courtesy in action and this builds the reputation of a nation. That is why people trust UAE as whole.

Finally whether a country or a company or an individual- your action speaks for you and only that alone can build reputation and earn people's trust.

You need to become a trustworthy neighbor too

"Trust is the natural consequence of promises fulfilled, of predictions that come true, and of values lived."
– **Helio Fred Garcia**

Let me narrate an incidence- experience that I had to go through. I bought a house in a housing society some years ago. Everything looked good, the property was good and to our liking. After a year or so I realized that internal roads were not being maintained and after rains, pot holes started appearing all along the road. When I enquired, I was told that this was an internal road and society has to maintain it and Municipal Corporation is not responsible. I wanted to know why was it not being repaired by the society?. They said there was no fund for this.

So I asked why don't we all contribute to the society fund and get the job done. All the residents told me that they did not trust the society chairman/caretaker and they know he will take the money and do nothing thereafter. So there was a huge trust deficit. I then decided to involve a few neighbors and create a small action group of like-minded people. We went door to door and most people said they would be ready to contribute as long as we do not involve the untrustworthy officials. I asked why they trusted us and we were told that our overall behavior and conduct was good and that is why they could trust us.

We collected money and a created an informal corpus and made a brand new road. As the plan rolled forward, a couple of civil engineers from the society came forward to help us select the right material- it was a cooperative work which worked on pure trust amongst neighbors.

All of us face problems in housing society meetings where people make noise and create ruckus for small meaningless issues. People living in homes, flats costing 4 to 5 crore Rupees squabble and argue for even 500 rupees! People don't trust the managing committee which only they have elected.

Winning trust is not difficult provided you have the right intentions

When I took charge as the head of a B school I wanted to connect with our alumni who were now working in the industry. Till then there was very little being done as the institute was just four year old. The students had created a small alumni association which limited its activities to send birthday greetings to alumni through mail- this was just of cosmetic value.

I wanted that we should have alumni get together and organize a dinner in cities where we had maximum numbers of ex-students. The funds were limited and a dinner was a bit of a stretch. I did not want to ask the alumni to contribute because it is human nature to first 'mistrust' and some one could say 'hey, the college wants to extract a party out of us because we are earning today'. This is generally the mindset and I will take this with a pinch of salt. Therefore I decided to have a meeting with the alumni team and put forward this concern. 'Can we call the entire alumni base and give a party? We need to fund it ourselves. How to do it?'

I trusted the students and asked them to make a detailed budget and see if we could do it. We dug deep and we did it. The alumni party was funded without charging the alumni, of course on a frugal budget, but it worked. The next year too we did it. Now something happened at that party which was a turning point for this exercise. One Alumnus came to me after dinner and said 'Sir, we are so happy that the college is calling us for a party and laying out a lavish dinner for us and not charging us even one rupee. But sir now we all are earning good money and why don't you allow us to contribute too?'

The trust was now established and the alumni themselves decided to contribute to the get together from that point on and a healthy workable trust based tradition started.

Every day is a learning

I worked for Symbiosis University for a decade. If someone asks me what is the secret of success of this organization- a spectacular success at that- I could sum it up in three words 'Trust based autonomy'.

Dr. S.B. Mujumdar the founder of this great institution gives the heads a total free hand. Every head feels that he owns the system, he feels it to be his own. This is a great feeling- owning it without owning it! There is no bickering or nagging on small things at all. One feels so oxygenated and energetic as you don't have to keep looking for approvals. You have a budget which you bid for and then you run the show- it is your show. The next budget meeting there is hand holding and no one is there to grill you for the sake of it. Minor aberrations, errors and omissions are ignored or set aside. I once asked him as to how he doesn't get concerned with these things and how he gives so much of financial freedom? His answer was that if he becomes a hawk and keeps worrying about small things and keeps pestering people to save say INR one million, what will he achieve? 'I will save a few lakhs but look at the damage it will do to the initiative and enthusiasm of the team- which is priceless!' Bingo, this builds trust- extremely pious trust. People are good and they reciprocate. Yes there is an audit but that is focused on financial bungling, fraud and misappropriation. I wish organizations learn this. Micromanagement and mistrust can totally demoralize an organization.

I can say with total conviction that out of my forty years of working life these ten years were the most fruitful where I enjoyed working and I delivered every bit too.

> 'Your personal brand serves as your best protection against business factors you can't control.'
> – **Dan Schawbel**

Involving stake holders

Alumni get together and alumni meets are great but I went a step ahead. I wanted alumni to be a part of our selection process and invited the senior guys to be part of the interview process! It generates tremendous respect both ways. They feel the college from where they passed out trusts them to this extent and they bring a lot to the table with their experience and knowing what we teach they can suggest changes too.

I ask the senior alumni to act as mentors and adopt two students each for industry mentoring. The communication is so easy today that it works very well and smoothly. I started a journal and annual business forecast where alumni contributed in terms of knowledge tremendously. This builds a very interactive trust based, mutual respect based bond.

> "The best way to find out if you can trust somebody is to trust them."
> – **Ernest Hemingway**

FAP- IIT Loans to students by Alumni association IIT Bombay

I am a part of IIT Bombay Alumni association. This is a unique organization run by the alumni and we have a CEO who sits in an office building within the Institute campus. One day as we were discussing certain issues I was told that one of the missions of this association is to give education loans to those students who crack the entrance exam but cannot afford the fees. I was told that no one ever defaulted paying back.

This is called FAP - Financial Aid Program

FAP is a broad based program that provides financial support for the entire registration fee of students including tuition fee, mess bill etc. FAP also provides support for equipment like laptops etc. as well as foreign travel.

This program started as legacy project and is one of the most successful alumni "giving back" initiatives supported by IITBAA (IIT Bombay Alumni Association.) and IITBHF (The IIT Bombay Heritage Foundation) was established as a non-profit public benefit corporation and received its status as a tax-exempt organization from the IRS.

Students are requested to donate back the funds received once they secure a job, for the benefit of future students, thus keeping the endowment perpetual and growing.

It is an honor based system, based on trust. Financial assistance is NOT a loan and there is no interest payment associated with it. Proactive student friendly approach, it has raised $50 Million

(INR 400 crore) from 3300 donors. It has benefited 5000 students.

> *'No one has ever become poor by giving.'*
> **– Anne Frank**

Money is not locked up in endowments with only interest available for use. Instead the entire sum of funds is available for students, increasing the 'velocity of money'.

Force multiplier effect not only positively impacting lives of many students but also creating a future generation of engaged alumni (having directly benefited from alumni support).

Any IITB student is eligible for this program.

Applications received around the year. They are vetted by IITBAA staff and interviews are conducted with the help of alumni.

Feedback by a beneficiary

"I was a recipient of the Financial Aid Program (FAP) during 2008-2009 academic year. The program supported my stay at IIT Bombay including tuition and hostel fees. I came from a remote area of Odisha and did not have any other financial support during the crucial final stages of research. This was an interest free financial assistance and I paid the amount immediately after I started working. The seamless process, the warmth and support of the Alumni Association that was helping me get FAP remains with me as a great memory. Therefore, after graduation I decided to do my very small bit in the FAP scheme and help IIT Bombay touch other lives like mine. I wish FAP many more successful journeys in future".

Small things matter too

In my opening address to a new batch I always emphasized on trust and made the rules of conduct very clear. I said 'I will trust you till you break my trust' and 'You will have to trust me that I will do everything in your interest and will never break this promise and never let you down' Hereafter the two years went on smoothly. I am humane but I am a hard task master and very strict with students as well as staff.

At the passing out closing address I used to square up things by saying ' Whatever I did was for your good, if I had been harsh or dealt with a strong hand with any one, there was nothing personal, it was for your good again'. This worked well- communication at the right time, the right way works very well- as long as you mean what you say.

One has to advise appropriately without holds barred. I remember a unique case where four students got an opportunity to work with the district administration in the North East. They were to work directly under the district collector and do a study of the efficacy of district welfare programs. These boys were really enthusiastic and full of excitement to go for it. Since I am familiar with that area, where number of illicit jobs are done by organized gangs who can be dangerous to deal with; I called these students and told them not to be too enthusiastic and go beyond the mandate given to them by the collector. I said your safety is of prime concern to me, though the administration will take care of you but you got to be cautious and careful and don't act in any rash or exuberant way that could harm you.

Once they returned after their project they came and met me and thanked me for the advice as they did see several things on ground which were not as per the rule book.

> *"If you can't communicate effectively, you will not lead."*
> **– Helio Fred Garcia**

Staff tea breaks- no town hall required

Another small initiative I started was to have a monthly staff meeting where right from the peon, lift man, janitor and all the teaching and non-teaching staff had a cup of tea or a simple meal together. We would exchange ideas and suggestions in an informal way and it created warmth and a bond based on mutual respect. I never really had to have a town hall meeting to address any issue.

In the army units there is a tradition to have a central tea break every day in the HQ where all officers come for a cup of tea. This is mandatory and gives the Commanding Officer an opportunity to see everyone at least once a day.

Never ignore someone in distress

It was an annual ritual for me to go and meet and interact with the industry who were our recruiters. It was just a courtesy call and meetings with HR heads and CEOs. It gives you broad sense of which way the industry and economy is moving. It was also meant to gauge manpower requirement of these companies and how that would impact our placement scenario.

One of the software companies which was our regular recruiter was not doing too well and in fact was laying off people. They were in a way caving in. When I told my student coordinator to fix up a meeting with their CEO, he said 'Sir they are in a bad shape, will not come to the campus and will not recruit a single student then why waste our time?' I responded 'That is precisely why I want to meet the CEO (who by now had built a good relation with us) as they are not doing well'.

> *"Lots of people want to ride with you in the limo, but what you want is someone who will take the bus with you when the limo breaks down."*
>
> **– OPRAH WINFREY**

When next day we met the CEO he was pleasantly surprised and said 'I am glad you came to see us, when we are going through a very bad patch, today everyone is ignoring us, no one comes to meet me!' There was a sudden bright spark in the student's eyes as eureka dawned on him. Now he realized why I insisted on that meeting. So do not betray friends basis their down fall. It doesn't matter how they fair in future, your character must always be consistent.

Chatham hall rule

Many people do not know about this rule- it is a code of conduct which works like an honor code.

When a meeting, or part thereof, is held under the Chatham House Rule, participants are free to use the information received, but neither the identity nor the affiliation of the speaker(s), nor that of any other participant, may be revealed. So everyone is free to speak his/her mind without inhibitions, as long as you follow this rule. This is done in a homogeneous setting where participants know each other's antecedents and can be trusted.

Even the high and mighty were ignored sometimes basis trust deficit

At the beginning of Second World War Albert Einstein learnt that Germany was working on creating a nuclear bomb so he wrote a letter to then president Roosevelt urging him to start building one for America. United States entered the war in 1941 and started project Manhattan involving thousands of scientists and technicians to build a bomb. Yet Albert Einstein was kept out of it because he was too outspoken and left leaning.

U.S. Army Intelligence office denied Einstein the security clearance needed to work on the Manhattan Project. Hundreds of scientists on the project were forbidden from consulting with Einstein, because the left-leaning political activist was deemed a potential security risk. The government could not trust him to keep it as a secret.

Trust pension or trust corpus

Once you have helped people and built trust on mutual respect it becomes like a bank deposit and earns you a life time reward. It may not be money but your one word becomes a command for those who trust you. Some of my past students still consult me regarding their professional choices, invite me for their wedding ceremonies and discuss even financial matters.

Sometimes they request me to be a referee and want to give my name on their CV. They trust me that is why they come.

Not only students, my old staff too sometimes consults me on even personal issues which they hesitate sharing with others. This gives you tremendous satisfaction and joy and you feel 'I must have done some good things back then'. This is the biggest reward you can ever aspire to get.

> 'To have compassion for those who suffer is a human quality which everyone should possess, especially those who have required comfort themselves in the past and have managed to find it in others.'
>
> – Giovanni Boccacci

Kiran Bedi

She became the first woman in India to join the officer ranks of the Indian Police Service (IPS) in 1972 and was the 24th Lieutenant Governor of Puducherry from 28 May 2016 to 16 February 2021. She is definitely a youth icon and I remember a couple of occasions where I interacted with her and students loved to listen to her. She released one of my books for which I am obliged.

She is the one who is a trusted person, dependable and forth right. She does not mince her words at all. Hundreds of IPS officers who retire as DGPs but no one is remembered and let alone revered by people as she still is.

Whatever task is given to her, she gives her 100% and her endeavor is to do – do something good even if she has to break the status quo.

Her Tihar Connection

Kiran Bedi took over Central Jail Tihar in 1993 in Delhi. It is the biggest jail in the entire South Asia with a capacity of 7,000 inmates. Such postings are considered as punishment for highly placed officers but she made this into a success. The work she did for uplifting the condition of the prisoners gave newer heights to her career and for that she won Magsaysay Award in 1994, the highest honor for a police officer of Indian Police Force.

She transformed the jail that was considered living hell for the inmates before she started her reforms. The jail filled with smugglers, rapists, murderers, drug sellers and dacoits besides terrorists and ISI agents were more like terror to staff of the jail those were hard to control. She changed the life of inmates of the prison with her humane approach and willingness to help them.

Education Initiative

She started with the education for inmates by making it mandatory for all. Everyone had to spend two hours in the morning for learning. The educated prisoners were appointed to teach the uneducated ones. The inmates willing to study further were provided with facilities to continue their further studies. Many prisoners benefited by this facility by becoming graduates from Open University. An under-trial prisoner who was there for more than 10 years was provided the library facility to learn criminal law to help in their legal procedures later.

Work for Prisoners Welfare

She concentrated on working conditions of prisoners to provide them better facilities related to their working opportunities inside the prison. She arranged exports of the cloth produced by prisoners that brought better price.

Inmates were trained in repairing works and provided with opportunities to get outside jobs that brought enough revenue to be distributed among the prisoners. All these activities brought her to headlines of national newspapers to be hailed by politicians and public alike. Different ministers and leaders of various parties visited Tihar to inspect and praise the Tihar's progress. All dignitaries those visited Tihar were all praise for the positive changes in the prison.

To improve the situation she found newer ways and most of these were different from the beaten track. For instance, she started a local level committee for women prisoners who would decide about small finance related disputes or bringing forward their demands before the jail administration thus far these never reached up to jail authorities. Now, their issues were taken care of on priority and promptly. She appointed a petition officer to bring the demands of the women prisoners on priority basis to her for her personal intervention. It was never done before in any Indian jail and was much appreciated. The best part was the violence that was regular feature of Tihar almost stopped. A two way trust was established.

Her firm conviction was that the aim of the police and jails is to remove the crime from the society and not the criminal. Mostly the role of police is limited to catch the criminals and get them punished and once the criminal is out of the jail, he repeats his crimes and comes back to jail because he does not know anything else to do.

If a criminal is repeating his crimes, it shows that the police failed in its purpose of removing the crime. Catching a criminal and jailing him is not a solution unless a way was found to stop his further involvement in crime by providing him a chance to do something worthwhile that will make him useful for the society.

She provided them a basic platform to learn and earn. She believed that jail was a hospital for criminals where they could get rid of their illness of criminal activities. Since the prisoners have to follow certain rules so they can learn to live within control, policing and lot many things that will convert them into good human being she introduced several new activities. It is not necessary to abuse them but they can learn through meditation too. Learn how to earn money while in the jail and make it a profession when out of the jail. If you will treat them ruthlessly, they will become more violent and feel lesser for the humanity and will head for further crimes. She thought to change them a humane approach was necessary and she was doing just the same with absolute dedication and honesty. She tried to make their life as normal as she could keeping rules of the jail intact.

She did not consider Police as a force that was created to punish the criminals but for her it was for the sole purpose of reforming the criminals. Jails were not concentration camps.

They should be more like schools where criminals could be converted into good citizens only if the police behaved with more humane methods. This was especially true for our country because most of our citizens have a trust in their religion. Religious methods work wonders on our prisoners. Meditation camps are working magic on most of the inmates and religion does not matter to them while going for meditation.

Kiran Bedi converted a jail into an 'Ashram' rather than an ordinary prison where violence was order of the day.

This huge effort and a unique approach earned her trust of her team, the society, the nation and most of all the inmates who now lived a better life with hope.

> *"The best and most beautiful things in the world cannot be seen or even touched. They must be felt with the heart."*
> **– Helen Keller**

Questions to answer

1. Why trust is important in every profession? Explain with examples.
2. List five attributes/qualities related to trust.
3. How helping others builds trust?
4. What do you understand by 'Never ignore someone in distress'?
5. Can one win trust of criminals and the debauch?
6. What do you understand by 'trust pension?'
7. What goes into making a good, sellable, acceptable brand?
8. What do you understand by Chatham hall rule?
9. What was Manhattan project?
10. On what basis Albert Einstein was not taken for Manhattan project

CHAPTER 6

THE LEVELS OF MILITARY TRUST

The safety, honor, and welfare of your country come first, always and every time.

The honor, welfare, and comfort of the men you command come next.

Your own ease, comfort, and safety come last, always and every time.

— **Field Marshall Philip Chetwode**

Trust lesson for life

Before I turn my attention to and talk about generals and field marshals let me begin with my academy days as a cadet about to be commissioned as an officer in a few months. You learn about competence faith and trust right from the grass root level and that principle remains perfectly applicable at all levels throughout your service and even beyond.

We have an exercise called '*The great escape*' where the entire course of more than 300 cadets is taken at night into the thick forest. You do not know where you are. You are stripped off your compass, maps, lighters, torches and money. You have nothing to eat that can be carried with you. It is a survival exercise too. You are left in twos in the thick of the forest and you have to reach the academy by hook or by crook undetected. There are traps laid on vantage points where instructors are tasked to ambush and catch you. One full battalion of professional soldiers is deployed to catch you! Once caught you are arrested and you are out of the game. Those who reach undetected are successful and are rewarded. This is the most exciting exercise at the end of our training.

Here people eventually catch up and a few groups get formed- not more than five because a larger group is easily detectable and difficult to hide. Which group you chose to join is crucial to your escape. People gather around a guy who they are confident of – you trust some of your batch mates who can be banked upon to negotiate the route to victory and finally escaping the clutches of mock enemy who is ready to ambush you on the way. This is based entirely on trust you have on the instantly chosen, identifiable and available leader on the spot- you do not have too much of choice and time is of essence too.

> '*The day soldiers stop bringing you their problems is the day you have stopped leading them.*"
>
> **– Collin Powell**

Basics remain the same even in high places

Here I would like to quote General Collin Powel the Chief of Army of US Army and later appointed as Secretary of State from his address to his staff at the state department and present a few relevant excerpts.

"That is exceptionally profound, and I've never forgotten it, because it means that we may not be sure, exactly, where you're going. We may be a little confused. We may be tired. We may be afraid. We may be cold. We may be hungry. We may want to be anywhere else on earth but with you right now, but we will follow you just to see what you think is around the corner. And why will we follow you? Because we trust you – we trust you with our lives. We are prepared for you to take us into battle. Follow me. Trust me."

He goes on about trust and leadership which are intertwined.

"My own personal definition is that leadership is the art of getting people to do more than the science of management says is possible. There are lots of variations and corollaries on that. Good leadership is getting people to do a lot more than the science of management says. If the science of management says that the capacity of this organization is at 100 percent, good leaders take it to 110 percent.

> *'Perpetual optimism is a force multiplier'*
> **– General Collin Powell**

You have to be people-centered. People are the followers. At Fort Benning, Georgia, when you go to the infantry school and you drive onto the base, the first thing you will see in front of the headquarters building is a statue. It's called "Iron Mike." And it's a statue of an infantry lieutenant, an infantry officer, who is posed with a rifle in one hand and he is pointing with the other hand.

And the motto of the infantry school, beneath the statue, is there, and there is no infantry officer or soldier who doesn't know what it is. It's "Follow me." That motto means: I am the leader. You are the follower. "Follow me." I know what I am doing. I am in charge. I am going to take you into the darkest night and bring you out safely. "Follow me."

So it's all about people, how you interact with people. The single word that captures what leadership is really all about and how you know when you have it and when you don't have it is the word "trust." Leaders have to be trusted by their followers. Leaders also have to be good followers. If a leader is a good follower, then the person above you, your leader, has confidence and trust in you.

The above discourse is the essence of foundation of trust. It indirectly flows out of confidence in the competence of the person you wish to follow.

> *Because the crew was convinced that I was "on their team" there were never any issues with negative criticism... You as a mentor have to establish that you are sincerely interested in the problems of the person you are mentoring.*
> **– Ret. Capt L. David Marquet,**
> *US Navy, and author of Turn the Ship Around!*

Back to the ground

During commando course- one of the toughest in the Indian Army- each trainee has to jump from a height of around 30 meters which is around hundred feet. This is scary and first an instructor demonstrates the right way of doing it to you and then he leads you to do it yourself. This is called confidence jump and once you finish it successfully you do feel elated with a feeling 'I did it'.

There is another exercise or jump which is one of the most grueling obstacles on the commando course. Trainees climb a four-story tower by grabbing onto the above platform and hoisting themselves up. The obstacle is so brutal because once they reach the top, their forearms are totally tired from previous wall climbs, rope climb. Once at the top of the tower, there is an instructor who attaches a rig with a ring and you jump and slide down yelling and splashing into water pool below. The instructor is also hanging at 100 feet but instills confidence in you so that you take the plunge. Those ten seconds are enough to make or break the trust in the instructor who finally pushes you down. Here also trust is very re assuring.

Field Marshal S.H.F.J Manekshaw

He took a hit of seven bullets, defeated death as a young captain, and rose to become the Chief of the Indian army, and after the victory of 1971, was made a Field Marshal.

Sam Manekshaw as he was popularly known, was able to demand courage from his soldiers because his own was never in doubt and he had amply demonstrated it on the battlefield.

Manekshaw commanded great respect worldwide in the military world which was bestowed on him when he visited Nepal after liberating Bangladesh, by King Mahendra, by conferring on him the title and sword of Honorary General of the Royal Nepal Army.

He always fought in his unique way for what was due to his troops and this is something that is withering away in modern armies.

An incidence worth narrating:-

Once there was a cut in the soldiers' uniform allowance. He decided to take matters into his own hands and invited the members of the Pay Commission to his room. He was impeccably dressed, as always. He walked up and down in his room pensively as if thinking something deeply before uttering anything. After some time, he turned to the members in the room and said "Now gentlemen, you tell me, who would obey my orders if I was dressed in a crumpled dhoti and kurta?" Such were the tales of Sam Manekshaw's ingenuity. Thus, the debate on the uniform allowance came to an end. Such actions win utmost trust.

Soldiers talk about his leadership, integrity, courage, and professionalism as a soldier. These were the values that Sam wanted the army to have and not be corrupted by external agencies and politics.

> *"Be an example to your men, in your duty and in private life. Never spare yourself and let your troops see that you don't in your endurance of fatigue and privation. Always be tactful and well-mannered. Avoid excessive sharpness*

or harshness of voice, which usually indicates the man who has shortcomings of his own to hide."
– **German Field Marshal Erwin Rommel**

Delegation earns trust

In May 2017, the Army News Service (US) published an article titled "Future warfare requires 'disciplined disobedience,' Army chief says." The article is a play on one of the six principles of mission command: exercise disciplined initiative. The premise of the article, for which the author interviewed Army Chief of Staff Gen. Mark Milley, is that future, complex battlefields will feature dispersed and disconnected small units operating to achieve common objectives—and that junior leaders will be required to make rapid decisions, within their commanders' intent, in order to preserve combat power, accomplish the purpose, and defeat the enemy. Gen. Milley made clear that commanders must not only convey tasks to subordinate leaders, but also the purpose of those tasks. This builds confidence and trust.

Moreover, he continued, leaders, even junior leaders, on future battlefields will be required to understand this purpose, and must have the competence to know what right action must be taken to accomplish not just the task, but the purpose, and the confidence to do what is right to accomplish the purpose.

The junior officers leading the operations need to win 100% trust of their men so as to come out successful.

How a general remembers a Field Marshal

Lt General A. S. Kalkat was army commander & former commander Indian Peace Keeping Force (IPKF), Sri Lanka and he recalls the way Sam Manekshaw came to them on the western front during the war with Pakistan in 1971 when he was the Chief and Kalkat a Lt Col.

'I remember an incident in December 1971, he recalls, which underscores the rapport the army chief had with his men and his indomitable valor.

We were deployed in the Chhamb sector where the most ferocious fighting of the 1971 Indo-Pakistan war took place. While the operations against the Pakistan army in East Bengal (now Bangladesh) were launched by the Indian Army after Pakistan's atrocities against the Bengalis in East Bengal and everyone's attention was on it, Pakistan launched a pre-emptive attack in the Western Theatre in Chhamb.

By now, it was a full-blown war on both fronts. Pakistan had some initial successes due to the surprise factor and overran the Indian brigade defending Chhamb. By this time, the Indian Army had reacted and deployed the 68 Brigade occupying the East Bank of the River Tawi. While the Tawi was not deep and the infantry could wade through it in most areas, there were only two possible crossings for tanks near the Chhamb Bridge over Tawi and the other about three kilometers south opposite a village called Darh. My battalion was deployed to defend the Chhamb crossing and another battalion was deployed to defend the Darh crossing. I had already demolished the bridge so that Pakistanis could not reach us.

Consequently, the divisional commander ordered me to launch a counter-attack. I launched the counter-attack soon after sundown in the darkness and after very fierce fighting and heavy casualties on both sides we succeeded and drove the Pakistani forces back across the river Tawi. The progress of our action was being monitored by an anxious army headquarters and the chief of the army staff General Manekshaw was informed immediately. He was away at the Eastern Theatre overseeing the operations against East Bengal which led to an eventual surrender by Pakistani army.

That night the Pakistanis attacked Darh with tanks and after fierce fighting, they were able to establish a bridge head at Darh by the morning. Pakistan was rapidly building up more forces in the bridge head during the day and it was assessed that during the night they would be able to have sufficient forces to launch a thrust towards Akhnoor about 25 KM east of Chhamb where the bridge over the Jammu Tawi was located. Its loss would have severed the eastern part of Jammu and Kashmir (J&K) from India and enabled Pakistan to attack Jammu from the rear, thus cutting off J & K from India.

The first thing the next morning, Sam Bahadur was with us. He had come personally to compliment the soldiers for their brave actions. He insisted on going right up to the forward positions. The subedar sahib cautioned that going up to the forward positions would draw enemy fire, especially if they had any inkling of who was in the field. Sam nonchalantly waved aside the objection saying: "Don't worry, let them know that I am here. They wouldn't want to tangle with me. In any case, they are bad shots and will probably miss me." Then striding forward he looked back at the subedar sahib and said with a twinkle in his eye. "Now, you be careful, sahib, they might get you instead." With that, off we went to the forward positions. The Pakistani soldiers were still on the ridges above and looking down at us. For whatever reason, no one fired even one shot. Throughout the light-hearted camaraderie of those hours with Sam, the men could see the steel behind those green eyes and it left them with renewed resolve and hope. This is how trust is built. If the leader is tough and brave the followers also get charged up and are ready to follow.

Powell on Trust

General Powell was the most respected and trusted Chiefs of US Army.

He tells a war story in brief.

"I was a battalion commander in Korea. As I was walking across the battalion area one day and I saw one of my soldiers walking by and he was down, he looked depressed, he was all dressed in his greens. It's his formal uniform, as opposed to his work clothes.

I said: "Hey, son, where are you going?" He replied: "I'm going back to the barracks, sir. I've just been over at brigade headquarters."

"Doing what?" I asked. "Well, they sent me over there to compete for Soldier of the Month to see if I can win being soldier of the month for the battalion, my battalion, and they had sent me over there to compete."

I said, "Well, how did you do?" He said, "Well, I didn't do very well. I came in third."

So, I said, "Well, when did you learn that you had to compete?" And he said, "Well, they didn't tell me until last night." I said, "Thank you, son, for representing us," and then I went back to our headquarters, and I went nuts. I got all of my commanders together. I said, "We will never, ever put a soldier in my battalion in that set of circumstances again." If it's important enough for us to do and participate in, then it's important enough for us to invest in the people that we are asking to do it. You should never set up anyone for failure, as long as you have the ability to do something about it. He links it to his staff in the State department as secretary of State and tells them: - And that's why we have fought so hard for resources. That's why we have fought to get the Diplomatic Readiness Initiative put in place. That's why we have fought to get our Information Technology up to speed. That's why we have fought to get the Overseas Building Offices program squared away, so that we're giving our people the equipment, the skills, the resources they need to be successful, so that they *trust us* when we send them out. Know your people, take care of your people, and it begins with training them.

It also begins with recognizing and rewarding them for good performance. It also includes professional development to make sure that people are promoted. It also involves discipline. An organization that is undisciplined, where people who are not performing get by with it – that is, continue their non-performance – is an organization that is not running at full RPM. It's not going to get that 110 percent that I'm looking for. I'm looking for more than 100 percent.

And so discipline is part of it. And it's also the toughest part of leadership. Nobody likes to look someone in the face and say,

"You're not doing the job." Or, even worse, to look someone in the face and say, "You're not doing the job and we can't improve you, we can't fix it, you've got to be moved." That is about one of the hardest things that one has to do as a leader and a manager. But it has to be done if you're going to keep the organization vibrant, if you're going to have a level of trust within the organization.

> *"A true leader has the confidence to stand alone, the courage to make tough decisions, and the compassion to listen to the needs of others. He does not set out to be a leader, but becomes one by the equality of his actions and the integrity of his intent."*
>
> **– Douglas McArthur**

Every time I have faced this over the years where, you know, you couldn't look away from a problem any longer and you couldn't fix it, you couldn't manage your way out of it, and finally you had to take that kind of action, it was difficult, it was painful, but I always found that afterwards, everybody else in the organization was waiting for you to do it. Each of them knew it long before you did. And what each of them is doing is sitting around saying, "How come that person's getting over and I'm working like a dog and the boss is not doing anything about it?"

If you don't, people stop respecting you and eventually you lose on trust.

Leadership is intensely personal. In my view, it comes down to a matter of trust, it comes down to a matter of loyalty: loyalty to each other, loyalty to followers, loyalty upward to leaders – loyalty in all directions.

Trusting your weapon

A personal weapon, a rifle or a carbine is the most sacred thing for a soldier. If it fails him he is dead if he fails to master it he is dead again. He needs a reliable weapon to protect himself and to kill the enemy. It has to be fail safe- no compromise on that. Every soldier in the battle has to maintain his weapon, keep it serviceable and working wherever he is desert, jungle or snow- he has no choice. Only then he can trust his weapon. That is why you are taught to sleep with your rifle, eat with your rifle and have it next to you even while shitting.

My Rifle – The Creed of a United States Marine

This creed, accredited to Major General William H. Rupertus, USMC and still taught to Marines undergoing Basic Training

First published in the San Diego Marine Corps Chevron March 14, 1942.

'This is my rifle. There are many like it, but this one is mine. My rifle is my best friend. It is my life. I must master it as I must master my life. My rifle, without me, is useless. Without my rifle, I am useless. I must fire my rifle true. I must shoot straighter than my enemy who is trying to kill me. I must shoot him before he shoots me.'

Not only small arms, every weapon purchased or manufactured indigenously must be totally reliable as a lot rests on it. Your life and honor of your unit and your nation.

Yes you can do it

Military is an organization that gets things done by you which you could never imagine you could ever do.

During commando course, which I happen to do and mentioned in some chapters earlier is one of the toughest courses in the world- definitely the toughest in the Indian Army. When you are nominated by your unit you do some pre course training and the guy who had done it before you becomes your default instructor cum guide. Despite having done this when you land up for the course at the infantry school you are scared and not sure of clearing it. The bench marks are far too high for one to even fathom. One is used to doing a ten mile run in battle order rig which is 16 Kms. That is the maximum one had done till then. In this course that is the start point- a speed march which is a slow jog with almost 30 Kilos on your back! The screw is gradually tightened and next week you do 26 Kilometers, next is 32 Kilometer's and the grand finale is 40 kilometers. This itinerary is told to you the first day and most think of giving up the first day itself. But your honor cum ego does not allow you to back off. So all of us do it- like it or not- you have no choice. Here also you need to trust yourself and your instructors keep telling you that if 50 courses before you did it so can you! Once you do the 40 Kilometer you are almost dead. But you are alive to say 'yes I did it'.

> *"Leadership is the art of getting someone else to do something you want done because he wants to do it."*
> **– Dwight D. Eisenhower**

A similar incidence is narrated by General Powell of the US army and here it goes:-

I'll never forget, I was in a brigade in the 101st Airborne Division, and we used to go out and run all the time in the morning, great fun, and there was this one soldier I would catch up with every few days, and he just couldn't keep up. He just had said to himself that he couldn't keep up. And we said, "No, you've got to keep up. You're going to be part of this outfit, that's the standard you've got to meet and you will meet it."

And so one day I was running with him – this was when I was considerably younger than I am now and was able to do such things – but this kid was about 19 years old, and I took him – it almost broke my heart, but I forced him to meet the standard that day. And he was – the last 500 yards, he was complaining, crying, grousing, mad, you know, "Why are you making me do this? You're down on me. Why are you making me do this?" And then he crossed the line and he did it. You should have seen him. "Yes, sir, that was me, man!" He had to have a high standard. He never knew what he was capable of accomplishing until somebody put that high standard up there for him and pulled him across it. That's what leaders do. And when you do that, you create a bond of trust between leader and follower that will not easily be broken. This is building trust in action. We are all then bound together by trust forever.

General George S. Patton, U.S. Army- was a unique leader who built trust by leading from the front.

Patton's leadership style can be best summed up in his following quotes which remain remarkably relevant to this day: "Do everything you ask of those you command." Patton believed leadership was done from the front, he understood that no one would follow a leader that didn't know what the work was like first-hand; "No good decision was ever made in a swivel chair." He rightly said.

The second key element of my training in the Army with respect to leadership was "take care of your people." This is second only to mission. It means know your troops. It means take care of your troops. The simple reason is that they accomplish the mission. They are the ones who ultimately get it done, they are the ones who ultimately, in an infantry context, are going to climb the hill and say, "This is now ours. We won."

Building trust with commitment

> *"No SEAL will be left behind"*
> **– Basic Principle of Navy SEALS**

When any military operation takes place, there are bound to be casualties and also on occasions there are people who get severely injured in any encounter. A soldier going into battle gets so much of comfort in his mind if he knows his comrades will never leave him behind for the enemy to kill, capture or torture him. He also knows that even if he is killed in action his dead body would be carried back home.

In the U.S. Armed Forces, they don't leave anyone behind. It's one of the basic pillars of what the Army calls the Warrior Ethos: "I will never leave a fallen comrade."

The U.S. military has made a sacred commitment to leave no one behind on the battlefield. This ethos is even embedded in the Airman's Creed ("I will never leave an airman behind") and the Soldier's Creed ("I will never leave a fallen comrade")

The 1998 movie "Saving Private Ryan" is one of the all-time Great War movies made by Spielberg.

The theme reflects the ethos of the army, where an American mother loses four of her five sons in the Second World War and the fifth one is also in the thick of the battle somewhere in Europe. The war department comes to know of this and reflects on the situation where they say 'How can we let a mother lose all her five sons in war? We have to get the fifth one out of danger and bring him home'

While much of the movie is a fictional account, the premise behind Capt. Miller's mission in the movie is based on a true story. That is the story of the Niland brothers — Edward, Preston, Robert, and Frederick — from Tonawanda, New York. Though operations need a soldiers to kill but they too are humans and have a heart. Bonding and commitment is too strong and builds a tremendous camaraderie and trust.

> *"Dependability, integrity, the characteristic of never knowingly doing anything wrong, that you would never cheat anyone, that you would give everybody a fair deal. Character is sort of an all-inclusive thing. If a man has character everyone has confidence in him. Soldiers must have confidence in their leader."*
>
> **– General Omar N. Bradley**

Trust and rules of the game called war

War is an ugly business- yet nations go to war with each other for national interest or political compulsions. Major casualty of any conflict are the armed forces personnel of warring nations and in the crossfire the civilians also get caught and suffer.

To protect uniformed fraternity/personnel and civilians the world required some rules and regulations on humanitarian grounds. Geneva Convention was a largely accepted frame work based on 'mutual trust' to protect people participating in war from inhuman treatment. For instance if enemy soldier lays down his arms and surrenders, you need to take him as a prisoner and not shoot him down- simple.

The Geneva Conventions are a set of several treaties, and three additional protocols, that establish international standards drafted as legal documents for treatment of soldiers on humanitarian grounds in war. The Geneva Conventions extensively define the basic rights of wartime prisoners, civilians and military personnel, established protections for the wounded and sick, and provided protections for the civilians in and around a war-zone. Treatment of PW or Prisoners of war was an important aspect of these regulations. It was the Third Geneva Convention. Most nations followed it and many did not and hence post such wars trials were conducted for those who violated these. Nuremburg trials against German war crimes in World War 2 are a testimony to this fact.

Man has from ancient times tried- yes tried to look as fair as possible. Idea was to instill some kind of fear of God.

In old Hindu religious scriptures it was hinged on a pivot of righteousness.

The levels of Military trust

Dharma-yuddha is a Sanskrit word made up of two words: dharma (धर्म) meaning righteousness, and yuddha (युद्ध) meaning warfare. In the Hindu Scriptures, it refers to a war that is fought while following several rules that make the war fair.

For instance, in a righteous war, equals fight equals. Chariot warriors are not supposed to attack cavalry and infantry, those on elephants are not supposed to attack foot soldiers, and so on. The build-up of weapons and armies is done with the full knowledge of the opposing side and no surprise attacks are made. Here also if your chariot is stuck in slush, and you are unable to defend yourself, the enemy is not supposed to attack you.

The rules of engagement also set out how warriors were to deal with noncombatants. No one should attack an enemy who has temporarily lost or dropped their weapon. The lives of women, prisoners of war, and farmers were also sacred. Pillaging the land was forbidden.

Dharma-yuddha also signifies that the war is not fought for gain or selfish reasons. A dharma-yuddha is waged to uphold the principles of righteousness.

Yet people frame these things or makes rules to break them. That is why the quote 'Everything is fair in love and war' - how convenient.

Questions for you

1. Why an extremely high level of trust is required in the armed forces between the leader and the led?
2. How is this different than trust in corporate world?

3. How do seniors establish and maintain trust with their team members?
4. You have to earn trust in the army, you cannot demand it. Explain in 200 words.
5. Why a personal weapon so important for a soldier?
6. What do you understand by "Do everything you ask of those you command"
7. What do you learn from the story of the film 'Saving Private Ryan'?
8. How can civilian organizations learn from armed forces and imbibe some ethos to build trust amongst employees?
9. What is Dharam-Yudh and how does this reflect in Geneva Convention?

CHAPTER 7

PATIENCE IS THE KEY TO BUILD TRUST- STEP BY STEP

'The key to everything is patience. You get the chicken by hatching the egg, not by smashing it'
— **Arnold H. Glasow**

Patience is the most important quality of a man or an organization to build trust. You build trust with people, one on one and also with other organizations you deal with. In fact you build trust in an ecosystem and the environment you operate in.

Trust as I mentioned in an earlier chapter works at an emotional level. That is why it is nurtured and cultivated over a period of time. There is no 'instant trust potion' that can be served in a cup. It is very gradually built. When a building is built, it takes time for the foundation to be created and mortar to set. Each slab is laid once the slab below it has been 'cured'. You have to water the cemented portion for days together to get it right. Similarly, Human bonds of trust are cemented with utmost care and curated over time. One should not attempt to make a reputation quickly. Advertisements can inform others of your brand but for people to accept it would take time. You need to invest into your trust building exercise and it is a constant conscious effort.

Faith, trust, respect and reverence are closely linked. You have faith in God because you trust him and that is why you revere him and worship him (highest form of devotion), you need to renew your faith by praying every day going to your holy place, a temple, a gurudwara, a church or a mosque to reaffirm faith and trust in god. In a crisis you fold your hands and say 'God help me' and hope is built within you and that gives you strength too.

Let us look at a few critical points to keep in mind to build trust.

1. It takes years to build trust but it can be shattered very quickly- today you can reach to your target audience through social media telling them about your strengths, at the same time social media acts like a double edged sword and your clients can write something against you whenever you are not up to the mark. In fact social media puts a lot of pressure today on every business.
2. Consistency is the key to keeping your trust intact. I call it as '99/1' syndrome in today's doubting society. People are unsparing and clients can be ruthless sometimes going overboard in criticism. You may deliver excellent 99 times

out of hundred but one bad performance can spoil the show. It also depends on the type of work you do but there are bad hits in almost every trust building exercise. You may take them as aberrations, but they stick out like a sore thumb in your profile. They are like weeds in the grass only thing is you can take out the weeds but cannot obliterate these from social media.

3. The best way to get around this problem is to accept your mistake say sorry and move on. Ensure you learn from the mistake. Sorry is a very powerful construct and makes the other person who is unhappy or angry to cool down. But avoid repeating the same mistake as repeating the same mistake several times is a sure 'trust buster'.

4. Remember; Trust= integrity and competence, intention. You must have spotlessly clean image and come out ten on ten on integrity. You cannot have any compromise on your integrity front. Similarly your 'intention' has to be truthful and on track. Whatever you do, do it sincerely and no one should be able to point a finger at you. Of course in business or work as an individual, your competence speaks for you. If you are a driver, you should be an excellent driver, If you are a cameraman you should be a sought after professional. For instance, I never default on or even delay my payments, EMI or any bills. This gives me a peace of mind and people respect that. I learnt in the armed forces almost for three decades that bouncing of a cheque could get into serious trouble and even a court martial. This good behavior and conduct gets so much drilled into you that you never default.

5. Promise less deliver more is very important, in fact is like a sutra or mantra to build trust. If you cannot do it don't

promise. You can politely refuse to take up the task rather than repenting later. You are labeled as a 'conceited, cocky or pompous'. You do this several times people will not take you seriously and that means a trust deficit.

6. Trust as by now must be clear plays an important role in every field. Whether you are doing stunts in a circus, or passing a baton in a relay race, or passing a ball to your team mate in soccer or you are a stunt director for a film, people need to trust you. If I in a football team know that I cannot trust my center forward to pass the ball at the right time for me to score a goal, the team can lose a match. Player's more than physical strength and coordination need each other's trust.

7. Trust earns respect. When you are a trustworthy person, everyone wants to work with you, all team heads love to have you on their teams, bosses respect your judgement and listen to your ideas and suggestions. In board meeting too this is reflected and it is equally important at grass root level. You respect a boss or a colleague whom you can trust for their judgement and overall performance. No one wants to work under an incompetent untrustworthy boss.

8. Avoid strong likes and dislikes. I have worked with such people who look at individuals in binary. You are either a one or a zero. Good or bad. And they make these impressions quickly and keep it lifelong. So if for some reason I am in your bad books, I will always remain bad. You don't give me a chance to improve- so why should I improve. And the blue eyed boys will always remain good. They can get away with murder as they say. The biggest loser is the organization if there is a leader like this. Because as law of averages, half

the organization is good and the other half is bad, black and white. Therefore the productivity of the organization also becomes just 50%. You do not trust your boss and your boss doesn't trust you with anything.

9. Follow through what you say. Do it and keep your promises. Many times leaders or bosses say something which is exaggerated or said for the heck of it (they don't mean it). This is a dangerous slope for any one. Even if said in a lighter vein people keep jeering you on one such point for very long. Case in point is the word uttered by a senior minister- Jumla- and it has become a part of the lexicon of the opposition in Indian politics. Firstly don't promise things- a reward or a punishment if you do not mean it (intention). But if you do then follow through and fulfil the reward or punishment. For example if you give a cutoff date to accept proposals, don't change the date under pressure or otherwise. People lose faith in the system and stop trusting you.

10. Olive branch works in case of a standoff. When egos are hurt and tempers are high people don't listen to reason. They dig in heels and there can be an expensive stalemate. Just to give a recent example of EUREA Europe, Ukraine, Russia, England and America crisis where nobody is prepared to smell the coffee. The whole world is suffering and a worldwide recession is looming large but no one is budging. If the two warring nations - Russia and Ukraine sit across the table and have some reconciliation and offer a peaceful solution it will be a win-win situation. Here also in international relations nations do not trust each other hence the problem.

> *'I come bearing an olive branch in one hand, and the freedom fighter's gun in the other. Do not let the olive branch fall from my hand.'*
>
> — **Yasser Arafat**

11. You can teach competence (IQ related) but can't teach character (EQ related) Character building is a mammoth task. It is not easy to teach in a class room. Only good character and transparent consistent behavior can earn respect and trust. A person can master Excel program but he cannot become a good character person through a few lessons.

12. Talk frankly- be transparent. It is better to be frank and be transparent in your dealings. This clearly shows your intentions are clear and you are not hiding anything from anyone. This builds trust on mutual basis. If there is a problem then say so- don't hide any facts.

These dozen points discussed above are very important to build and retain trust.

These need to be cultivated and one has to be at these constantly.

Bankability

I was talking to someone a few days back about his buying another property in Mumbai and suggested a friend who could help him in locating something good. He immediately responded

'I bought my last home through a broker and also rented my commercial property through him. He is very good and I fully trust him. I will go to him rather than any one.' Look at the power of trust, this property broker did a good job and built a solid reputation and basis that a permanent bond of trust. He would make trust his USP and will get repeat requests for his service.

Organizational politics- a sure recipe for disaster

I am a firm believer that politics starts from top and blame is put on the employees down the ladder. Top management's most important agenda and task is to build trust within the organization and for that you should have zero tolerance policy for politics. The top bosses must make sure to announce this (and practice too) during town hall meetings, team discussions, outbound and every opportunity to interact with people. Internal politics is like termite which will eat the organization from within and is a silent killer. An organization is so peaceful and productive where people would love to stay if there is no internal politics which invariably divides an organization into two or even several camps. It serves no other purpose more than backstabbing, bickering, bad mouthing and back biting making everyone's life uncomfortable.

Trust lasts long after you quit the top position.

This is a huge bonus. Once trustworthy, always trustworthy. I have seen and even experienced how trust never stops chasing you like good character even after you quit the top job. It is an honor and matter of pride if people still come to seek your advice in personal capacity after you have quit office. Trust builds on trust.

Trust becomes the product differentiator today

Product companies don't have a lot left unless they rely on relationships. Technology has brought product differential to a minimum; each product is as good as the other. There is no way to have the cheapest prices in the marketplace anymore because you are operating on very thin profit margins and high overheads. Therefore, high-quality relationships between you and your customers are a must to be successful. For instance there are hundreds of home delivery services after the pandemic it has become a way of life. The ones who have patiently built trust are thriving with customer repeats.

A major part of maintaining these relationships is patience. When patience between parties no longer exists, things are said that are often repented later. Due to emotional outbursts, these actions frequently destroy the relationships. This results in dissatisfied customers, unhappy sales teams and the profits and customer retention going down the drain. In this situation you lose customers, lose referral opportunities and lose revenue.

People which is your customer is impatient like a child who is like a cry baby. He cries, throws up his hands and shouts to dissuade other would be customers too. You need to handle these people with kid's gloves- patiently. They want everything good, hot and cheap and 'now'- now that is the problem. A guy is throwing tantrums you can't let loose your bouncers on him/her. You need to be tactful, polite and diplomatic to diffuse the situation, and it is not easy.

We need to remind ourselves that a lack of patience is part of today's lifestyle, and as salespeople, we must deal with that whether we like it or not- in hospitality the mantra has been 'guest is always right'.

Even project management and execution requires huge amount of patience. I have handled big technical projects involving millions and hundreds of people sitting in different locations- you don't have full control on several factors like suppliers, quality of raw material, external factors like weather, delays, laziness, irresponsible behavior be a few guys down the chain and hundred such problems. You cannot lose patience.

> *'Have patience. All things are difficult before they become easy.'*
>
> **– Saadi Shirazi**

Metro man

Unfortunately Public sector performance in India has been very poor since the time of our independence seven decades ago. People blame it on culture, lack of accountability and also lack of leadership. It has now for almost six decades become a de-facto standard and we almost gave up on this as a bad joke. There is a carrot but no stick. You require a carrot to motivate and a stick to prod. This is the way an average human works. We are ordinary humans too. But we require a messiah to change that and yes such people bring hope.

From building the bridges to railways of modern India for the past 60 years, the 85-year-old civil-engineer E Sreedharan has revolutionized the notion of public projects on multiple levels- speedy completion, minimal cost, quality results and all this with zero corruption. He fortunately got the support of a strong political will.

Some of his mantras to build trust and the first metro in the country are worth mentioning.

Communicate your vision-your grand plan

Let your people know what they are striving for. Make the big picture clear. Have a clear organizational culture. Delhi Metro Rail Corporation (DMRC) emphasized on integrity of the work and strict adherence to time. Choose your organizational culture accordingly and ensure whatever you choose, you implement it strongly.

Transparency is important

Transparency builds trust. Ensure that the employees feel that the system is fair and reliable. All DMRC staff took an oath of integrity before work to never indulge in corruption and report if such cases should arise.

Have systems in place for effective hearing of complaints and suggestions that can be used to improve the system.

He had his feet always on the street!

E Sreedharan took a daily round of the projects he was assigned upon to understand and be abreast of what the ground level progress was rather than hear status reports from his team. This avoided delays and all issues were nipped in the bud.

Care for people to earn respect and their trust

He as a leader expressed concern for those who worked 'extremely hard' and not giving time for their family. "I pity those who work for 18 hours a day," he said.

His three tips for leaders to achieve work-life balance

The Metroman's first tip for those unable to cope is to acquire skills of managing time. Second, he also advises them to learn the art of delegation of power. The third tip is to trust team members.

If you know how to delegate power and learn to trust your assistants, there will be ample time for everything," said the experienced engineer turned techno manager.

It took the government 190 km of this project roll out and 14 years to muster the courage to let him go. And yet, two weeks before E Sreedharan quits as managing director, Delhi Metro Rail Corporation (DMRC), their trepidation is palpable. The question is not whether Phase III of the Delhi Metro will be completed by its deadline. The question is whether it will be done the Sreedharan way. Will his legacy continue after he is no longer at the steering wheel?

The man himself is unruffled and confident about the system and culture he has created. He has full faith in his team to carry forward Delhi Metro's sterling tradition. After all, the credit for the project's success must go to the 7,000 employees who work hard every day, he says. This is Sreedharan the leader, who has evolved a system that he believes, can do without him. This is Sreedharan the man, who is self-effacing in his humility and can't be bothered with glory.

"When you delegate tasks, you create followers. When you delegate authority, you create leaders."

– **Craig Groeschel,**
The founder of Life Church

Questions to answer

1. There are twelve critical points discussed in this chapter to build trust. Which four according to you are the most important? Justify your answer with some examples.
2. Give an example of how patience becomes an important part of building trust.
3. How can you ensure that when you leave the organization, it still works efficiently?
4. Why do you think organizational politics is bad for organization and people?
5. How can you stop organizational politics?
6. Why trust becomes a product differentiator today despite so much being offered as product innovation and value addition?

CHAPTER 8

INTERNATIONAL RELATIONS AND TRUST

"Trust, but verify"

US President Ronald Reagan's signature phrase

The international political stage is much like a game of chess between multiple players. These players are not individuals or organizations but are sovereign states. All are independent entities as nation states or countries. A state or country which has sovereignty over a defined geographic area, is completely independent of any other country, and has its own government is termed as a nation state.

There are around 195 countries in the world and the smallest one being the Vatican in just 110 acres! The population too is just around 1000 people. The place is historically connected with the world's greatest artists like Michelangelo and Leonardo da

Vinci, and several others. Vatican is not a part of United Nations. Monaco is the second smallest country with an area of 1.98 km² with a population of almost 38,100 plus including residents from 125 nationalities.

Historical perspective Of International relations

The idea of inter- country/state relations and dealing of these independent entities with each other in a more organized way became essential when bigger nations became powerful and could wield pressure on others and influence either war or peace. The idea was born in the United States in the beginning of 20th century and got traction during and immediately after World War I. There was obviously a growing demand and efforts to find less-dangerous and more-workable means of conducting relations between peoples of nations, governments, and economies. Europe was next to get into this as the world went to war again in 1939.

Between the First and Second Word Wars the idea was to create international frameworks like League of Nations which could prevent wars by helping nations talk to each other through a notional nodal agency. World leaders wanted treaties and pacts between nations, open, transparent and open for everyone to see rather than being a closely guarded surreptitiously executed state secret. The basic germ of mistrust or mistrust bug was always there in each and every leader's mind after the First World War and remained alive and kicking through the Second World War with several pacts and treaties between nations being forged and broken at will.

After six years of war where millions perished, the world got divided in two camps one led by Americans (West) and the other by USSR (East) they became the Eastern and Western blocks with their own trusted allies. This remained a period of cold war where the trust was thrown out of the window and US and USSR kept a suspicious eye on each other right after the Second Word War was over in 1945. Spy agencies like KGB and CIA were fully geared up to spy on each other.

The United Nations was born with these big brothers controlling it. The cost of cold war was steep for both the blocks as both were building arms and nukes to protect themselves. They were also arming their allies to keep a balance of power in this sense of the term. Soviet Union disintegrated in 1991 and a bipolar world for a while became unipolar with captain America as the sole super power. As if in parallel other powers like China, Israel and India started forging ahead and the world became multipolar- each one flexing its own muscles to remain relevant and safe in this complex equation of nations.

At the heart of 'International Relations matrix' is the self-interest of every nation state- which makes sense and it is plain common sense. It becomes more pronounced because of the uneven level playing field for 195 nations. There are mighty nations, militarily, economically, politically, resources wise and then there are under developed poor nations on the other side of the spectrum who cannot even fight for their existence alone. The idea of National interest becomes the only and only construct of paramount interest to each country big or small. You got to survive at all costs.

National interest thus is the most critical construct/concept in international relations. It is the key concept in foreign policy of every nation as it provides the fundamentals based on which foreign policy is made. While formulating foreign policy, all governments are guided by their respective national interests. It is the purpose of foreign policy to conduct foreign relations to achieve national interest to the maximum extent. Though it is not easy to define or quantify what a nation's national interest is.

This ambiguity is caused by the different usage of the concept in different contexts. National interest may explain the aspirations of the state. It can also be utilized operationally in the execution of the actual policies and programs followed. It can be used aggressively in arguments to explain, or criticize an action.

Yet the idea of national interest is at the heart of explaining, predicting and understanding international behavior of state actors. From time immemorial, leaders of states justify their actions in the name of the national interest. For example Napoleon said he was acting in the interest of his nation when he initiated the Russian campaign. Later, he mounted a last desperate battle at Waterloo. Adolf Hitler justified his expansionist policies, including a mindless multi-front war, in the name of Germany's national interest.

Johnson and Bush were convinced that interests of US were at stake in the historical Vietnam War and Gulf War, respectively.

The bottom line is that nation-states' minimum requirement is to protect their physical, political, economic freedom and cultural identity against encroachments by other nation-states- bordering or far away.

From these general objectives, a state's leaders can take specific cooperative and conflict policy decisions, such as competitive armaments, the balance of power, foreign aid, alliances, subversion, and economic and propaganda warfare.

Function and Purpose of National Interest

As the overriding purpose governing the state's relationship with the outside world, it serves two purposes. It gives a general orientation towards the external environment. Also, it serves as the basic criterion of choice in immediate situations which need a response. It also adds an element of consistency in a nation's foreign policy and long term behavior. Governments change but national Interest remains a guiding beacon in a swiftly changing geopolitical situation to maintain a balanced approach.

Whatever ideological, moral, or legal standing a political party governing a nation has- a nation has to take decisions according to what suits its interest and in the best interest of its people.

> *'A diplomat is a person who can tell you to go to hell in such a way that you actually look forward to the trip.'*
> **– Caskie Stinnett**

The rules of the game

The rules of the game are that there are no rules of the game. You play along and keep fine tuning as the circumstances unfold. Yet there are serious and rational assumptions.

International relations, or anywhere that human beings interact, predictable behavior is essential for nations to steer on day to day basis. It is assumed that everyone will drive on the same side of the road and follow traffic rules to the tee. In the absence of this, driving would be very dangerous, and many of us would stop driving. It is taken for granted therefore that everyone will follow this rule because of obvious self-interest.

But it seldom happens like that again because everyone is selfish- no brownie points are required for a state, it needs its survival and the best for its people. In actuality there is an anarchy of sorts.

Yet trust lies at the center of strategies and policy making to deter and compel certain behaviors when dealing with friend and enemies alike. Yet there are no permanent enemies or friends much like politics. You play a game to win and not lose, yet you may give some grace marks to the others if you can afford.

People got to believe that you will carry out your spelt out threats and dig your heels if they do not comply with your demands. A nation must make its threats look credible and communicate accordingly.

Reputation is the most important parameter for trust, your credibility depends on a reputation basis your honoring your earlier promises. Today for instance no one in the world trusts China. People say that openly. Americans are also very clever and ruthless. They con others into such commitments which suit them but care little for others. A case in point is Ukraine Russia war.

Henry Kissinger once quipped that *"it may be dangerous to be America's enemy, but to be America's friend is fatal."*

It can be assumed that "crime pays". Invasion, backstabbing, letting down and cheating in arms control or trade agreements result in significant advantages. Ukraine is now trapped by America cheered by Europe. America is selling its arms to them and egging President Zelensky to fight till the last man! Not even one American soldier has died but thousands of Russians and Ukrainians are dead. US is selling its oil like never before and whenever the war ends it will draw out contracts to re build Ukraine again sucking up their economy. US wants Russia to weaken at the cost of Europe indirectly and Ukraine directly and sitting pretty thousands of miles away egging the world, escalating the conflict. One theory may harm Europe in the long run- all the mercenaries and unemployed soldiers with weapons and ammo in their hands will create havoc and devastation in the entire Europe- after all it is a continent with small countries.

The latest one in the hat is 'that Ukraine will not get NATO membership!' Wow what was this war about?

This plays out as a game of billiards- you hit a ball to hit another ball which hits another ball to pot another ball! Or try a 'cannon' shot to score points indirectly. Great players use a rebound from a cushion cleverly to surprise the opponent by doing the unthinkable!

In such a messy affair it is a tight rope walk for every nation and difficult to remain neutral, yet credible and most difficult to build trust.

Pakistan has always betrayed India and if one can say backstabbed India several times. It has never abandoned a proxy war against India through terrorism. Yet there were constant efforts from

Indian side to build confidence through confidence building measures.

Another game of billiards is being played by America. It is propping India to check China and propping up Pakistan to check India. Bravo.

You got to trust but not blindly and yet keep an eye on the events and happenings in real time. This oxymoron reflects that agreements and treaties can be valuable but may not be always kept of course they are comforting..

There are no gentlemen in this game. Yet there is a constant endeavor by diplomats and top political leadership to project an image of 'holier than though' in front of the entire world community.

If all were gentlemen, politicians, diplomats and spies will be out of business.

As I write

As I write this book, this chapter by the end of 2023, India is making great strides and the world is watching us carefully. Some big powers who have been used to the idea of an entitled pecking order are feeling the heat and not liking it. India doesn't exist in vacuum and has to thrive amongst the sharks. It has to play its trust and diplomatic cards very carefully, smartly and quickly. We have won the trust of nations with plain speak. India has not taken sides as far as Ukraine-Russia-Europe-America (UREA) conflict is concerned. Yet a polite but logical and firm stand regarding energy imports in the national interest has gone a long way in messaging the right vibes. India has won trust of nations like Japan, Saudi and UAE at the highest level of political pyramid.

We used goodwill to take out our stranded students from the war zone- again friendship and trust came handy. While the so called all mighty US, hoarded the vaccines during the Covid crises India helped the smallest of the small countries by giving vaccines to them.

India has yet proven that despite good gestures, do help and one can stay on course even if you help others in whatever little way you can. We have built a reputation. Our PM and External affairs minister have done a great job and are making India a nation to reckon with.

Why nations do not respect their treaties.

Treaties are meant to be broken!

Why nations negotiate and sign agreements promising to act in a way when they have no intention of following these? Reasons or excuses can be several. Leaders may undertake commitments under duress and hope like hell to wriggle out of these promises later under better circumstances in the future.

Versailles Treaty after WW I was signed by Germany because it was cornered by the rest of the nations- Germans who had lost the war had little or no choice. It grossly violated all salient points regarding the size of its army and its weaponry as soon as it could get away with it.

Circumstances can change, making freely negotiated agreements no longer appear to be good deals.

John F Kennedy protested in 1962 against Russia deploying nuclear weapons and its military presence in Cuba. Today Joe Biden is doing just that with Ukraine by egging it to join NATO so that it can expand its footprint nearer to Russia. Things change, value change with time. And now the US and its gang of EU are looking the other way- wavering on NATO membership to Ukraine!

In conclusion I would say that building trust amongst nations is a huge challenge and every nation especially the less powerful are always on a slippery slope. The more powerful don't care and they more often than not get away with even murder.

As they say 'show must go on' and as a metro or a big city never sleeps (work is always in progress).At global level it would be fair to say 'the world never sleeps'

'You aren't going to be successful as a diplomat if you don't understand the strategic context in which you are actually negotiating. It is not deal making. It's not.' Condoleezza Rice

Questions to Answer

1. What do you understand by 'National Interest?
2. Why is National interest important for every nation?
3. Which country is the most trusted by others according to you?
4. Do nations follow the rules of the game?
5. Why are treatise signed if they have not to be honored later?

CHAPTER 9

MEDIA AND TRUST

"Until you realize how easy it is for your mind to be manipulated, you remain the puppet of someone else's game."

– Evita Ochel

Media is changing colors like Chameleon today

The fourth estate or the fourth pillar of a democracy itself is under fire across the world and since it is changing its shape, size and color so quickly, it is not only surviving in front of a firing squad but thriving too. It is like the terminator or predator of Hollywood fame- you can't beat it ever.

Media a plural of medium is the means of communication, as radio and television, newspapers, magazines, and the internet, that reach or influence people widely. This is a huge platter!

There are two major reasons for its changing roles and its power. Influence by technology and also by several other external factors.

In earlier days people were used to a couple of newspapers, a few magazines and a local radio station. Let me add- and everyone was happy. Then came the TV and satellite and last two decades the internet and mobile communication. Because of a good business opportunity they became multiple channels in every sphere of influence and that too very rapidly.

Today even in India you have hundreds of TV channels, Hundreds of radio stations, Thousands of newspapers and magazines in several local languages and English. Coupled with apps and social media the information flow is nonstop- much higher than what a human can absorb.

These technologies have flooded the information and mind space so rapidly that the mind of an average news consumer has gone numb. A news reader, presenter or an anchor has become like a cyborg. He now has several wires attached to him/her and something plugged in the ears too. If he turns there is a small device on his belt at the back right above his bum. These are visible to you but you cannot see several Teleprompters which he is constantly looking at to get his cues. A living robot.

Media has become therefore a MBRL- Multi barrel Rocket launcher which can pulverize a target on ground in minutes.

Multi mingled mind

Any citizen basically requires news to understand and know 'what is happening'. Instead he is overloaded with news and repeatedly bombarded with so much of information which could be fake, wrong, and unnecessary or even biased that the basic purpose of news is lost. News is no more news. It is a mind managing tool. It has become a tool for propaganda. The word propaganda emanated from propagation.

Propaganda is a modern Latin word, meaning 'to spread' or 'to propagate', thus propaganda means for that which is to be propagated. Originally this word derived from a new administrative body of the Catholic Church created in 1622 as part of the Counter-Reformation, called the Congregatio de Propaganda Fide (Congregation for Propagating the Faith), or informally simply Propaganda. Its activity was aimed at "propagating" the Catholic faith in non-Catholic countries.

The term began taking a pejorative or negative connotation in the mid-19th century, when it was used in the political sphere. Therefore religion and politics both got linked to this idea making the things murkier.

The second issue therefore is the external pulls and pressures emanating out of its usage for influencing human minds. Since media is a mind manipulating machine it wields tremendous power. An old term 'information is power' (meant you hide information and don't let others access it) also now means disseminating information is a bigger power.

Everyone or anyone who wants to capture the imagination or more truly make you imagine the way he wants, would like to control it. Therefore politics, religion, clout, industry, geopolitics, money power and advertisements are the major stake holders. Actually there is a race to produce MORE NEWS THAN the actual NEWS. This stems from the fact that there are far more ways of communication than you really require.

The control system

Within this giant wheel there are several wheels. The controlling people are the state (Some channels directly) the industry, money power, the religious powers that be and the intellect. Though media is free!

The state cannot let go its stranglehold, it is a part of their job to regulate for the good of the citizens. So there are lines and guidelines not to cross those lines. These lines are not written on stone but sometimes on shifting sands. We all know sands shift according to the winds which are not static. Therefore these lines change according to which side the wind blows- in fact media is so powerful today with a vice like grip on billions of minds that it can itself change the directions of the wind!

> *"Just because something isn't a lie does not mean that it isn't deceptive. A liar knows that he is a liar, but one who speaks mere portions of truth in order to deceive is a craftsman of destruction."*
>
> – Criss Jami

Dire state of affairs

Today there is a trust deficit in every field. Executive, law makers, even judiciary is not spared. Law enforcement agencies like police or investigating agencies are also under public scrutiny. And all this is supposed to be brought on your table by media. So how can media be a holy cow? First of all it is not a cow, it is men and women who run it. It is the man behind the gun- here in front of the camera.

Whenever there is human intervention you ought to give a margin of not error but a deliberate twist as human minds are twisted or can be twisted. Therefore media which itself can be manipulated is manipulating your minds! To trust media- any media- becomes difficult. No wonder more studies are coming out with this malice. "Americans' Trust in Media Falls to Record Low" says Gallup Survey.

Stats about media stats are also given by media! Advertorials and paid reviews are not uncommon.

People love to hear what they love to hear to reinforce their beliefs. This is another twist in media's tail.

If I am left thinking type then I will tune into left oriented channels and if I am right thinking I will never watch left oriented channels.

In any case trust has been declining steadily for decades, and the real reasons have to do with economic and technological changes in the industry itself, not with a single controversial politician or fleeting partisan dispute. While there are always a few bad apples, the vast majority of working journalists simply want to inform the public and hold the powerful people accountable regardless of political affiliation.

Internet made things very complicated for the public and the prosecutor or the politicians too.

Bill Clinton's affair with Monica Lewinsky, was outed online by Matt Drudge, a 31-year-old gossipmonger and former CBS Studios gift-shop T-shirt vendor working out of his Hollywood apartment.

Since this story turned out to be true — and dominated headlines for a year and led to an impeachment — gave Matt Drudge a kind of 'rogue validity', even though his avenue rarely did any actual journalism but simply aggregated some sizzling headlines from elsewhere, and even though its hammer head "scoop" didn't involve reporting but simply the unauthorized publication of someone else's reporting. The event led the public to think of unfiltered online gossip publications as potential news sources and romanticized the idea that anyone with a computer could become a citizen reporter. Today videos going viral and counter allegations have become a trend all across the world- you can brain wash any brain in a matter of hours.

Internet did far more damage to journalism in terms of revenues which mainly come from advertisements. Not only news but advertisements which migrated to sites such as Amazon, flipkart that offered wider exposure at cheaper prices. This was like a blood bath and as they say 'survival of the fittest', in this case it had to be survival of the smartest. Before long a large number of local newspapers folded or were sold to chains or to hedge funds and other businesses that were not primarily news organizations.

TRP was the name of the game for TV channels and the more you excite the viewer the more enticed he/she is to latch on to you hence better advertisement rates for shorter slots.

In such a dog eat dog scenario how can one expect a saint to run the show?

> *'We all need money, but there are degrees of desperation.'*
> **– Anthony Burgess**

A Reuters report finds that "large minorities" in some countries "have very negative or cynical views about how they think journalists do their jobs, including allowing personal opinions to influence coverage, accepting undisclosed payment from sources, or deliberately seeking to manipulate the public."

Public is, entitled to decide whom to trust for news and current affairs national or international. A generation back, most Americans said they trusted the network news shows with their iconic anchors, and their local newspapers to tell them the truth about the daily news. Obviously that trust has declined, even as more and more sources of news and information have emerged. A wide gap in trust has emerged across ideological and political lines, especially after the presidency of Donald Trump who renamed the news media "fake news." At the beginning of the book I had said that today over all trust within the society at large has dwindled and that is why in every sphere of profession there is a 'integrity deficit'.

In fact fake news has also become a soap factory and there are fakes and counter-fakes floating across on the net like debris in the space, which one comes in your orbit is difficult to say. Headlines can twist a tail/tale. Vested interests and invested interests do matter in this jigsaw puzzle. For an end user it is nothing short of an information deluge, some genuine some fake. AI needs to invent a "FAKOMETER". Some say that Artificial Intelligence (AI) will create such a genuine looking fake news that you will not be able to find the truth ever!

"Repeat a lie often enough and it becomes the truth", is a law of propaganda often attributed to the Nazi leader Joseph Goebbels.

Among psychologists something like this known as the "illusion of truth" effect.

Remember this was around 1940 when the medium of communication was largely radio and newspapers/posters and films to some extent.

Today reverse can also be true 'you repeat a truth thousand times and still it remains a lie' –thanks to multiple sources of media- multimedia.

Let me give an example from Electronic Warfare (EW) as today for a consumer media is nothing less than info warfare which he has to handle himself.

Basically there two facets to it, ECM and ECCM

An electronic countermeasure (ECM) is an electrical or electronic system designed to trick or deceive radar, sonar, or other detection systems, etc. It may be used both offensively and defensively to deny targeting information to an enemy. The system may make many separate targets appear to the enemy, or make the real target appear to disappear or move about randomly to confuse the enemy.

To counter this scientists and engineers came up with ECCM. Electronic counter-countermeasures (ECCM) is that component of electronic warfare which includes a variety of methods and gadgets which aim to reduce or to some extent eliminate the effect of electronic countermeasures (ECM) on electronic sensors aboard vehicles, ships and aircraft and weapons such as missiles.

One size does not fit all; you as a consumer can do, as many channels/publications do- segmentation like covering, politics, economics, crime, entertainment, editorial. Finally a viewer has to take his own call, use his gut feeling and common sense to an extent- whom to trust or not. Who speaks and who carries the news still matters and that could be a rule of thumb for anyone to make an informed decision-tune in or not.

> *'To a man with a hammer, everything looks like a nail'*
> **– Abraham Maslow**

Social media has a new dimension- catharsis

Earlier media was one way- the controller/editor/regulator could censor and then transmit or propagate. Social media is like a sledge hammer in the hand of every living human being! The levels of frustration can be seen in social media posts. People can go over the top and abuse anyone. It is like a safety valve for many but a danger to the society.

Whats app has given a new dimension to venting feelings – memes, short videos and jokes can change/influence opinions. Earlier people would say statistically, or logically speaking today it is 'whatsappically speaking' some call it whats App University in a humorous way.

Post-truth

Post word refers to 'after' as in post-operative care

This is a relatively new term being used by the media intellects. For general public which simply seeks the truth from media this can or may cause some confusion.

Truth has long been one of the prime and serious concern of public debate. Post-truth is about a historical problem regarding truth in everyday life, especially politics and governance.

Post-truth is a term that refers to the 21st century widespread documentation of and concern about disputes over public truth claims. The term's academic development refers to the theories and research that explain the historically specific causes and the effects of the phenomenon.

While the term was used academically before as post-truth politics, later it was popularly defined it as "relating to and denoting circumstances in which objective facts are less influential in shaping public opinion than appeals to emotion and personal belief." Largely because of multiple sources.

For example in its most potent and virulent mode, post-truth politics can make use of conspirational mode. In this form of post-truth politics, false rumors (such as the "birther" or "Muslim" conspiracy theories about Barack Obama) become major news topics.

In recent years the western media is coming hammer and tongs after India regarding freedom of speech and minority rights when they have no business in any nation's internal affairs. Yet they are hell bent on creating a narrative of their own.

> *"There was a time when we used to have opinions, just humble opinions. Now everything seems to be a question of life and death. We defend, we abuse, we call names, we shout….is it because every idiot in town suddenly found a voice through social media or are intelligent people getting*

dumber trying to defend arguments which an idiot won't understand. I don't belong to either so I just wonder..."
– **EverSkeptic**

Role of Artificial Intelligence- aka AI

In recent years AI is making news for several reasons. Though still in its nascent years, it also has invaded our minds as some enigma which will change, alter create and destroy our lives (so many pundits talk about it- many not clear themselves of what it is). No doubt it has potential and far reaching impact on everything yet only time will tell. One of the simplest and most straightforward definitions of AI was presented by John McCarthy, a professor of computer science at Stanford University, as "the science and engineering of making intelligent systems." The intelligent systems could be in the form of software, hardware, or a combination of both.

As far as media and news is concerned it will do the dirty job of cleaning the muck created by so many channels and back channels due to business needs and technology push.

AI algorithms can effectively scrutinize and analyze vast amounts of data from various sources and check whether the news is correct. This helps journalists to produce honest and unbiased news.

The India scene

With a huge 1.4 Billion population and 60% out of that being young and aspiring – it is the Kurukshetra for media conglomerates.

Indian media has grown into an economic juggernaut, with a revenue turnover far exceeding one percent of the national gross domestic product (GDP) and is equivalent of the size of many individual industries/verticals in India. It is said to be the most dynamic media industry in the world and one of the fastest growing. The media's worth is equivalent to half the value of India's famously successful computer software exports.

Media in general and especially in India faces a serious crisis of credibility, most people don't trust. Without public trust, reliability, the Indian media will cease to matter to large numbers of people except as a source of cheap entertainment, unnecessary worthless excitement and titillation.

The silver lining is that trust in news has grown amid the coronavirus pandemic with 44 per cent of the respondents globally saying they trust most news most of the time, but the figure is below average at 38 per cent in India, according to a survey.

Despite humungous growth in the media industry, the lack of quality and conviction shows a serious disconnect with the real lives of people in the country and the day to day issues they face. What sells is politics, cricket and anything controversial regarding faith and the latest being gender bias and government bashing!

Yet people respect and care about legacy print brands running for decades and government broadcasters like Doordarshan and All India Radio are more trusted, while print brands, in general, are more trusted than TV brands, which are seen as far more sensational and full of rhetoric.

Personal experience

I have been writing books and articles/columns for some esteemed publishers and newspapers/magazines.

In addition several of my books have been reviewed in very reputed publications and papers. My experience has been that there is a fair play. If your stuff is good then you get your due. I found editors very honest and professional. I could extend that to news too but not very sure of that.

> *"People shouldn't expect the mass media to do investigative stories. That job belongs to the 'fringe' media."*
> **– Ted Koppel**

Questions to answer

1. Why do you think there is so much clutter in media today?
2. What are the basis and meaning of propaganda?
3. What is the best way to verify news?
4. What is the role of AI in restoring faith in media?
5. What do you understand by post truth? Give an example.

CHAPTER 10

BUSINESS TRUST

'Trust is like a glue that helps keep business and customers together'

A good boss is an anti-attrition glue as people don't quit jobs but they quit bosses. Similarly a good organization has to be a trusted organization to keep all the stake holders on board.

The stake holders

Running a business is much more complex than working for someone. In a job you do your job, you have a job description, you have limited role and responsibility. Whereas, as a business entity you have to constantly watch several things simultaneously. You deal with several sub entities to run the show. You cannot just focus on one and neglect the others. For instance some organizations may just focus on customer care and neglect the vendors. Some may look after the interest of vendors but neglect its people. You may look after the people but neglect your product. The list goes on.

To simplify things, let us look at who all matter or who are the stake holders?

The major stake holders are, your customers, the human resource, vendors and suppliers, the top management, and your product. Broadly there are entities within and also outside the organization. And let me divide these in two compartments. As a business entity you must win trust of all stake holders.

- *The ones outside the organization*

These are the customers, your vendors/suppliers, the regulators, the Government, the law enforcing agencies and the law.

- *Those within the organization*

Your people, your hardware, machinery and finally what matters the most is your product.

Importance of trust in Business and workplace

Trust is a single point business maker or business breaker. Lack of trust is your biggest expense which you may not be able to reflect on your balance sheet. All things equal, this is the most tangible yet very intangible asset of an organization which ultimately creates a brand. Let me remind you that no brand guru or brand building agency can build a better brand than the organization itself. Without trust, transactions cannot occur, influence is destroyed, leaders can lose teams and salespeople can lose sales. The list goes on. Trust and relationships, much more than money, are the currency of business.

Brand is not a logo but a whole lot of sentiment attached to it- trust is the strongest asset of an organization.

The markets are getting crowded and competition becoming more and more fiercer, brands have starting to understand that trust becomes a major differentiator that makes or breaks a brand or your name in the market. Marketers realize and understand that brand's ability to deliver on promises, create consumer experiences and provide value to its customers consistently through its product and services are factors that make a brand stand out.

You at the end of the day exist because of the customers you serve. They pay for your product or service you offer and out of that money you are able to run your business and create wealth for your entity and employees.

When people spend their money with you, they're placing trust in you and your business. If that trust is lost, the customer is likely to be lost and you may lose other customers too - your reputation travels by word of mouth. Today it travels at the speed of light because mouth not only speaks (sound) but also coveys it on the internet through social media. What took a year earlier may take just a few hours to spread. Good as well as bad.

Unfortunately today a customer is spoilt for choice. He has so many mind bogging offers for every product that he is looking for, that finally and eventually he bets on his trust. Very simple- if I cannot trust you why should I come to you?

If trust is lost in personal relationships with family and friends, people are much more likely to work hard to rebuild it. If trust is lost in a customer to business relationship, people are most likely to just move on.

Trust energizes an organization and acts like oil to smoothen things and make things move faster

Within the organization it is mostly the people who take decisions, confer with each other, decide things and take actions.

If people doubt each other's intentions, their game plan, agendas and their capability how can they work smoothly- in fact how can they work at all? You can have long meetings, discussions and debates and presentations but if there is always a doubt in each of the participants or the team members mind about the intent and integrity of the person sitting on the chair next to him- nothing will move.

If you reverse the situation and each member trusts the others then things will move quickly- you reach a consensus and take a collective call in a cordial manner.

The work gets done not only smoothly, happily but done at a faster speed.

It was often said that the bottle neck is always at the top of the bottle- meaning the top guy. But mistrust in an organization can make the whole bottle a bottle neck!

When there is an intra organizational trust the cost of decision making goes down and the speed of decision making goes up. When so much time is wasted on coming to a consensus- due to mistrust- you are missing the point 'time is money'. Your stress levels go up, your efficiency goes down and your salary is billed to 'lack of trust syndrome'. Due to mistrust most people waste time to convince others, rather than work on the issue at hand.

In simple terms trust is having faith and confidence in some one. For instance when you want to visit a doctor you take a feedback from your friends who have visited the same doctor earlier. In fact this feedback is to reinforce your trust in the doctor. If someone says 'Don't ever go to that dentist- you will get screwed' the dentist is screwed.

> *'The glue that holds business relationships together, that is trust, and this trust is purely based on integrity'*
> *– Brian Tracy*

Rapport is another way of looking at trust

Rapport, rapprochement or solidarity are feelings of comfort at personal level.

Rapport forms the very basis of meaningful, and harmonious relationships between people. It's the sense of acceptability that you get when you meet someone you like, and whose point of view you appreciate. It's the bond that forms when you discover that you share one another's values and priorities in life.

When you strike a rapport with someone you're both focused, and interested in, what the other person is suggesting, there is a mutual understanding which is also called chemistry in recent days. When you click with someone it is a feeling of trust. Your energy levels, tone and body language match up.

Such people are cheerful and happy with each other, and are concerned for one another.

The joint services training in the National Defense Academy where cadets from Army, Navy and air force are trained together for three years is basically to build a rapport, a bond for life and this works well into a battle field. Soldiers on ground trust their air force and know that aircraft for air support will come on time or a helicopter or a ship will be there to pick them up at the mutually decided place and time.

I feel companies should invest in such interventions to create solidarity and sense of belonging within employees. This can prove to be a very good asset in the long run. Knowing how to build rapport can help you to perform successfully.

Some people have it as a natural gift to get along with others, and some need to learn it.

Building trust is a constant effort like keeping yourself fit

Trust is the natural result of thousands of big and small actions, expressions, ideas, and intentions. Trust does not happen quickly; gaining trust takes hard work and nurturing. It is like nurturing a rose bed for a long time before you get flowers. It might take years of perusing a customer to break through and fully gain their confidence and trust. It requires tremendous patience and perseverance to gain trust. Yet in spite of the importance of trust in the business world today, few leaders have given it the focus and nurturing it deserves.

Six C's of Trust

These are character, competency, commitment, consistency, clarity and compassion

Let me explain each of these briefly.

Character – This word 'character' may sound old fashioned yet it is the most trusted factor or thread for trust and a time tested factor. Every one notices where you stand and for what you stand. People look for those who have basic human values- those who do what is right over what is easy and may be unethical. Your character is your reputation and your reputation is your long lasting asset, it eventually becomes a brand. The bottom line is your value system what you stand for. Are you consistent through thick and thin? Do you keep your word of honor? If yes I trust you. Simple.

Character is on top of the stack in terms of building faith.

Let me put this on record 'small things are actually huge'. People say 'missing forest for trees' I say don't miss trees looking at the forest to build character!

Small trees make a huge jungle- tree by tree- one day.

Let me illustrate by giving yet another example of TATAs a most respected company and a well-groomed family which has done a great deal for India and the society at large. This entire organization respects the armed forces like no one else does. It gives a substantial amount of discount on meals to all uniformed people. This looks like a small gesture but it travels far and wide.

Every drop counts. Come to think of it how much does it cost over a year to do this? It is not money it is the gesture that counts.

Fortunately character cannot be bought from the shelf of a super market! Like there is no price tag to your honor like a tuxedo.

Cost of an Olympic gold medal may be in hundreds of dollars but its value is priceless!

Competency – You cannot be delivering your promises if you are not good at what you are supposed to do. Your service or the product you produce can only be good if you know your work, you know your job. Therefore competence counts and it counts in a big way. Even if you run a small motor garage, people will watch how good are you? They will not even get the wheel alignment done from you till they are sure you know your beans. You will not go to a dentist who is not a good dentist- an incompetent dentist at that! Whatever your business – be the best, better than anyone else in the business.

Commitment – Unless people see commitment and passion in you, they would not repose their faith in you. Are you dedicated? Are you ready and committed to even take a loss and stand committed to your promises? These are rock solid traits. If you are committed and people perceive you like that over a period of time let me tell you that even if you commit a mistake (not deliberate) people will forgive you. That is the power of commitment to your customers and your cause.

Consistency – Now this is very important and a difficult thing to achieve. You are supposed to do the same thing over and over again with same enthusiasm, same dedication and deliver hundred percent in every case- in a way zero error syndrome. If you make burgers then your burger must taste as good every time I buy one. It must taste the same!

Yes McDonald did it. Ray Kroc bought the business from McDonald brothers almost at a throw away price. With his vision, commitment he built it into an empire which grew to nearly 35,000 stores in 119 countries. To build consistency into a massive multi location corporation, especially serving food – not shampoos- was a big task. But he did it. Restaurants were to be kept properly sanitized at all times, and the staff must be clean, properly groomed and polite, especially to children. The food was to be of a strictly fixed, standardized content and restaurants were not allowed to deviate from specifications in any way. There was to be no waste of anything, Kroc insisted.

Why its French fries were a hit? Consistence was the name of the game. Potatoes are the ingredient and no rocket science- but he gave it a shape of science and technology way back then in 60's. In order to reproduce the superior taste of these potatoes, Kroc devised a system using an electric fan to dry the potatoes in a similar way.

People love to see the little things done consistently.

> 'Consistency is the true foundation of trust. Either keep your promises or do not make them'
>
> **– Roy T. Bennett**

Clarity – Every organization must come clean on this aspect. People don't like fine print or to read between the lines. If there are too many * or ** and 'conditions apply' clauses people may get put off.

There should be no 'what's the catch'? Kind of feeling your brand must convey. Say upfront what you give and what you don't else you may attract only a one time customer.

People trust the clear and mistrust the ambiguous.

Compassion – Today organizations are spending a substantial portion of what they earn towards social responsibility. Climate change, green projects, empowering women and children through education, helping people start a small business. Customers at large have faith in those who care beyond themselves.

A story of compassion, humanity and great character

Zavere Poonawala is a well-known Parsi industrialist from Pune. He is brother of Serum Institute of India (SII) chairman and managing director Cyrus Poonawala.

Ganga Datt was his (Zavere poonawala) driver for thirty years and one fine day he passed away. At the time of demise, Mr. Zavere Poonawala was in Mumbai attending some official work. As soon as he heard the news of his diver's death, he cancelled all his meetings, requested the driver's family to wait for him for the cremation, and rushed to Pune by a helicopter. On reaching Pune, he asked his limousine car to be decorated with flowers as he wished Ganga Datt should be taken in the same car, which he drove for thirty years. When Ganga Datt's family agreed to his wishes, he himself drove Ganga Datt from his home up to the ghat (funeral place on the banks of river) on his last journey. When asked about his gesture, Mr Poonawala replied that Ganha Datt had served him day and night, and the least he could do is to be eternally grateful to him. He further added that Ganga Datt rose from the poverty and educated both his children very well. His says that we should always be grateful to those people who contributed to our success.

This is compassion and character in action.

Some Do's and don'ts

Admit when things go wrong.

With social media so active and kicking, it is almost impossible to hide today. You can neither duck nor pass the buck. If you don't admit your mistake be prepared to pay a heavy price and this could erode your well nurtured customer base. There are big car manufacturers who have called back millions of their sold out pieces to make corrections which could be attributed to manufacturing defect or an oversight. This would cost a lot but would ensure you hold your head high and face the customers confidently for your future business deals.

Promise less and deliver more.

This is a no brainer and a simple axiom to follow. Promise what you can do and don't give false hopes to your customers. For instance if a car gives 12 Km to a liter of fuel don't sell it by saying it will give you 15 Km to a liter. Someone will come back and punch you in your face. If you cannot finish your job in a week, don't ever commit. Ask for ten days and deliver before time and you will be rewarded big time. These are not estimates that go wrong, it is just over exuberance to attract customer's basis wrong intention.

Be transparent

When a property consultant sells you a flat, he must tell you upfront if there are any challenges or shortfalls in the property that you are buying. That is precisely the reason why people engage a consultant. Same goes for solicitors or legal experts. You must present a clear picture right from day one.

Accept if you are wrong

Facing your customer about why he no longer feels good about your business or product and taking it as a positive feedback builds trust. It is not easy because as humans we tend to take things personally and we can find it difficult to listen to criticism. Yet if you develop a positive mindset and project it as a positive trait you yourself will feel good and pat your back and say 'look I take criticism as a feedback or constructive criticism'.

Be sincere and genuinely concerned

Do what you say and say what you do. Trust can be eroded if you say one thing but do another.

If you tell a customer that you understand their difficulty but do not solve the problem, they will not trust you in the future.

Trust is a two way street – but it can work like magic in business

It is mutual- Normally people who trust each other walk half the way up to shake hands- the other half is done by the other guy. So do not expect the other fellow to do all the walking- it is always you give some and you take some. At the end of the day if you work with trust as the basis both parties end up feeling satisfied and happy with the business transaction. And this builds such a strong feeling that they are mutually attracted to each other to keep working in future too.

> *Trusting is hard. Knowing who to trust, even harder.*
> **– Maria Snyder**

Entrepreneurs and startups

A startup cannot start on a shaky wicket. Most startups start small and are short of funds. Hardware, infrastructure and people you employ cost money. Building trust does not cost you a penny. Therefore for an entrepreneur who is just trying to take off, trust becomes your trusted support partner- that is your biggest asset. You require wings to fly and trust in your clients will give you wings of fire.

Let me give an example; if you are an interior designer and take a contract to do up some one's home décor- don't try to make a big buck from the first guy. Create a big trust bank instead. Do your job to the Tee and deliver before time, keep the budget tight and deliver more than you promised- let me tell you your reputation will travel at a lightning speed. Today referral system is very strong because people don't trust adverts, they trust trusted friends. Therefore trust has a ripple effect. As a startup you must hit the bull's eye in your first job itself.

Trust is like integrity

If you have trust nothing else matters and if you do not have trust nothing else matters.

It is binary in a way. You trust or you don't trust- Like a woman is either pregnant or she is not pregnant, she cannot be half pregnant.

Business partners who trust each other spend less time and energy protecting themselves from being exploited, and both sides achieve better outcomes in negotiations. They eventually make a win-win situation for each other by design.

Rebuilding lost trust

Restoring trust is very important in any business once it's lost. It requires a big effort to rebuild trust. Especially with Suspicion Quotient so high in people today, it would require ten times the earlier effort you made to build trust.

When things go wrong, it can be really difficult to face the music. You are already losing business and in addition facing the wrath of public, customers and media in some cases.

We are inclined to hide and try to move on. But if you want to restore people's trust in your business, you're going to need to be brave and forth right. You need to take it on the chin.

Let me give an example of a film star from India, Mr. Amitabh Bachchan, who ventured into a business and lost big time. He had taken money from several people who leant him because of his status and respect. He was advised by some people to declare himself as bankrupt and be done with. He said 'People have trusted me and I cannot let them down, I cannot betray their trust.' He promised to return every penny back to everyone. His acting career was also looking southwards at that time, but he worked hard to bounce back to earn to repay his loans. He actually kept his reputation spotlessly clean. This demonstrates character which is one of the pillars of trust as discussed earlier. He didn't let down his friends and associates, in a way God rewarded him with such a long career- he is working even at a ripe age of 80 plus.

Walk the talk and then talk the walk

First you must walk the talk- do what you said. Once you have done it properly and earned a name it is time to talk about what you walked- not before. Talking the walk also is very important in business. If you have built reputation and trust with hard work, let people know it, of course good reputation travels as fast with word of mouth but no harm if you project your achievements to customers because today there is a lot of clutter in the market. India has had a very rich, and old culture and heritage. Unfortunately we never talked about it even within the nation. Instead of being proud of it we ourselves for God alone what reasons played it down.

Trusted companies-reputation and credibility

Today and may be for the last several decades business houses have been bench marked by organizations who do bench marking of companies. There are several parameters but one important one is trust.

The top five most trusted companies according to Infegy- which claims to be the most intuitive consumer intelligence platform available- are:-

1. HP
2. 3M
3. Gillette
4. LinkedIn
5. PayPal

The top most respected Indian brands are

- Infosys Ltd
- Tata Consultancy Services Ltd
- Wipro Ltd
- Tech Mahindra Ltd

'It takes two to do the trust tango--the one who risks (the trustor) and the one who is trustworthy (the trustee); each must play their role'

Questions to answer

1. What do you understand by building rapport?
2. Who are the major stake holders in a business?
3. List and explain at least five C's of trust.
4. Trust is like integrity- explain.
5. What do you understand by 'Walk the talk and then talk the walk' as given in the chapter?

CHAPTER 11

POLITICAL TRUST

*P*olitical trust, is generally defined as citizens' confidence in political institutions, and indicates political rightfulness, legality —the belief in the righteousness of these institutions, instruments of governance and the regime of which they are a part. It is a belief that institutions and processes are operating in good faith- the belief that leaders are acting in what they think are the best interests of people and the nation. It is often influenced by past experience with past governments. A constant comparison is obvious.

National interest is of paramount interest to political leadership- and should be- but citizens generally are interested in what good the government is doing for him/her, yet in today's connected world and due to impact of social media there is some kind of importance attached to national interest by population at large.

Trust is definitely an emotion that doesn't get enough credit for how intense and important it can really be. Trust is a feeling of confidence and security that a government cares. Trust is a complex neural process that binds diverse representations into a semantic pointer that includes emotions.

Trust deficit between the government and the people can be very dangerous and harmful for the wellbeing of a nation state.

Political landscape is very huge and complex today

Simply put, every nation has a different set of problems, different people, different aspirations and different governing models. Therefore 'one size fits all' for understanding or even dissecting the process may not be a good idea.

Today, despite its shortfalls, democracy is the de-facto acceptable political model across the world and every democracy is unfortunately clamoring to preserve other democracies! Every nation, which means its people at large and its duly elected government aka politicians are poking their nose in other's affairs.

Democracy is preferred because it 'supposedly' gives the people enough power to change the government itself and also allows a lot of elbow space for freedom – which could mean different things for different people.

Though Winston Churchill once said that: "democracy is the worst form of government – except for all the others that have been tried."

Whether it is the worst form of government or not, there is little doubt that the alternatives are worse. Suppressing people's views through dictatorship, military rule or tyranny means the rule of a narrow minority over the rest. Yet if you are strict with the people of a nation and you are well meaning and for the nation people will love you and trust you to the tee. Case in point is former PM of Singapore- Lee Kuan Yew.

Today governing has become very difficult

The basic reasons for this difficulty are media and public aspiration. In fact media helps catapulting a common man's aspirations as now he gets to see what others have- and he aspires for those things. He is no more a frog in the well- he may be in the well but he now has a periscope to see outside the well too. And that periscope is the media which also can show him what it wishes to, a deliberately tainted or skewed view suiting one or the other stake holders. Politics is directly impacted as a politician is now under twenty four seven scrutiny by the people. You don't have to wait for next day newspaper as everything is available on your palm top in near real time. At the same time media can play havoc in the minds of people by distorting facts and fake and counter-fake news is flying around in the environment all the time. Mostly unchecked.

Let us take example of one of the largest democracy and most diverse one- that is India

Nothing can be more complex than governing India for example. It is now the largest democracy in terms of number of people- 1.4 billion and counting. It has very diverse cultures and different languages.

A total of 780 languages co-exist in India. The constitution recognizes 22 regional languages. India has 29 states and 8 union territories. Cuisine and traditions change with each adjacent geographical location and the slogan 'unity in diversity' fits very well into this scenario.

India got its independence from the British colonial Raj in 1947 at a heavy price of partitioning of the country into two nations- India and Pakistan- sworn enemies from day one till now.

There are external major hostile nations like China and Pakistan which the government has to worry about constantly. It has long borders to defend and a huge coastline to look after and guard. The terrain varies largely with vast stretches of plains, rivers, desert, jungles and mountains.

The country was ruled by Congress- one single political party for well over 65 years and had several collation governments too. From 2014 till the time of writing this book in the middle of 2023, it now has one party majority government run by the BJP (Bhartiya Janta Party). A stable government is best for any nation state and that is what matters at the end of the day.

Faith verses Trust

A lot of people believe that these two words mean the same thing. Faith is more commonly used in a spiritual context while trust is an important concept in relationships. These two concepts go hand in hand and often refer to believing in something. In terms of relationships, faith leads to trust.

Faith in your government's intention and ability leads to a good foundation for building trust by the politicians or the ruling government in power. This trust is very important in times of crisis when citizens need reliable guidance and support from political leadership. For example, in the event of an epidemic or a pandemic like Covid 19 , which created worldwide panic and uncertainty, it is essential that citizens trust the advice of public health officials in order to protect themselves and their near and dear ones.

This happened recently and each government reacted differently as there was no past precedence to follow. Despite all the good intentions many governments came out with better results than others who could not handle this calamity effectively. Ultimately the people were at the receiving end.

This was an event that did help some political leaders in establishing good faith in the masses. In case of India, the political leadership took several risks to manufacture vaccines at home. They vaccinated crores of Indian citizens at an unprecedented pace and also earned good will in the entire global community by providing vaccines and medical aid to several other nations too- most who could not afford. This not only generated good will and faith in the geopolitical space but also helped Indians taking their self-esteem several notches higher.

Taking risks is risky

Yet in today's environment this is essential for good leadership. In political leadership the stakes are very high for the leaders as well as the people.

Under the leadership of Prime Minster Modi India managed the Covid crisis with whatever could be salvaged- there was no perfect solution which any one had to offer. No one claims it was great or even good.

He had the guts to take difficult decisions even putting his political existence at risk. With opposition, foreign media and several guys within the nation all watching like hawks and who are constantly looking for one single major failure by him or his administration so that he could drown or they can take him down. With such an environment, taking risky decisions is still more risky and requires tremendous courage of conviction.

Let me illustrate this with an example. Every safe flying trapeze rig in a circus has a large safety net underneath the ring. If an artist/gymnast misses a catch, or slips and falls off the bar, he lands on the net and is saved. In case of PM Modi the risks and stakes were higher than one could imagine, they had national and international ramifications and he did it without a safety net!

And people of your nation watch it too.

The entire opposition was asking him to go for importing Covid Vaccine and there was no point making our own. In any case someone will come out with one and all we need to do was to pay and buy!

He said this was the easiest thing to do but he wanted 'Atmanirbhar' Bharat- self-reliant India and went ahead with indigenous development and mass production of vaccines at home. He was candid enough to say and accept that he had put his entire political capital at risk- but he did it. Many opposition parties even had the gumption of reposing no faith in our own scientists and the ruling government!

Let me compare this with another event in the history.

When US president Truman ordered the atomic bombing of Nagasaki and Hiroshima, it was a tough decision—in fact, the toughest one for any president till date.

When Oppenheimer the scientist who made the bomb met the president after the bombing he expressed his anguish by saying 'I feel I have blood on my hands'. Truman responded by saying 'no one cares a shit who made the bomb, It is I who ordered it to be dropped'. He took the entire blame/credit for it. (As depicted in the movie Oppenheimer).

Ever since August 6, 1945, when the first atomic bomb detonated over Hiroshima, the human race has lived in fear of nuclear annihilation.

In the annals of history, few events have had more importance than this first atomic bombing, and no historical figure has been associated with this bomb more than Harry Truman, who commanded his military to use the new weapon less than four months after taking office.

In case of Truman, it was millions of Japanese that would perish due to Atomic bombing but in case of Modi, it was lives of his own people at risk- and that is the major difference.

All most all the members of his council of ministers say that the biggest strength of the Prime Minister was to take risks. This was one reason his team always stood by him. Yes this too built his reputation and trust and masses love him and have total faith in him.

He did several such things which he did with good intentions and in national interest in his two innings. The abrogation of Article 370 was like chutzpa moment for him.

The air strike on Balakot in Pakistan, Indian aircraft crossing the Line of Control (LOC), and going 80 km deep to bomb terrorist camps in Pakistan was a very tricky and risky decision too. Anything could have gone wrong—but he did it. The executive order was given by him. An ordinary man will not be able to sleep with this kind of stress. These actions of the government made his supporters coin a slogan 'Modi hai to mumkin hai' which roughly translates 'If Modi is there anything is possible' if this is not trust of the people then what is?

Trust is an essential component of a free, democratic society. Faith in the process of laws and elections leads to a decrease in violence, an increase in social programs, and a willingness to sacrifice temporary individual interests in favor of collective societal interests. Modi has been able to achieve this under the most trying circumstances.

Today people are watchful and are more informed

All the time good and well-meaning citizens always pray that the common man who votes can understand the difference between wheat and chaff- and so do the politicians.

One thing which must be mentioned is that the moment you change the status que and bring in new policies- those few who fall on the wrong side of the decision are bound to be hurt and hurl abuses at the politicians.

Yet at a national level, masses understand and appreciate progress and prosperity.

To build trust PM Modi built a lot of tangible assets in terms of investing in infrastructure, like roads, highways and laying optical fiber for digital India across the length and breadth of the country.

These are all visible initiatives. Perceived by a common man.

Those who do it build respect and earn trust

To build the nation at a faster speed and making several course corrections PM Modi built meaningful trust in the masses. Let me illustrate this.

We missed out on the first and second industrial revolutions. The first one was in Europe between the mid-18th and mid-19th centuries when India was under the British East India Company. The Second Industrial Revolution occurred in the 20th century, but then India was ruled by the British whose aim was to use India as a raw materials mine and as a market for finished British industrial goods. We were desperate for imported frying pans, toasters, mixers, cutlery, and bone china. An imported shampoo or aftershave lotion was a prized possession. All cars were imported and we were going gaga over Triumph, Harleys and BSA motor bikes and brands like Jeeps, Plymouth, Impalas, Hillman, Vauxhall, MG some British some American. People went abroad only to shop 'imported 'goods. Then there was a tsunami of Japanese brands like Kawasaki, Honda and Sony. We bought comforters and table mats from Dubai! We were going crazy and we were kept starved- I don't know why?

After independence we failed to industrialize unlike its East Asian counterparts. We chose a Soviet-style planned economy that was protectionist in nature. After Independence, Nehru our PM for more than 15 years attempted an industrial revolution via the state. He didn't trust private entrepreneurs, so he made the state the entrepreneur, and not surprisingly, he failed. Even then the government did not let go of its strangle hold on the industry with fixed Quota Raj fixation. British Raj left after 200 years and on came the self-imposed Quota Raj.

If you want to take just one country on the same time line as ours, it would be South Korea which was an underdeveloped, agrarian economy that depended heavily on foreign aid. It was governed for almost three decades by military government with an iron like grip yet a pragmatic governance model to improve economy. South Korean economy grew at an average annual rate of nearly 9 percent, and per capita income increased more than a hundredfold. South Korea was transformed into an industrial powerhouse with a highly skilled labor force. Hyundai and KIA are house hold names today in India- All South Korean cars dominate the market.

We had missed the bus in a big way just because of our wrong policies. Since providing service and making a buck is lot easier there is hardly any enthusiasm of even neo entrepreneurs for the manufacturing where you got to literally dirty your hands and sweat it out. Manufacturing is a tough nut to crack.

You can't create an industrial base in a jiffy. You need trained manpower, designers and right fit managers. No wonder our PM has emphasized on skill India to train artisans who are the backbone of any industry.

Today, India is growing rapidly and aspires to touch the $5-trillion mark. With strong global tailwinds in the future, India can embrace industrialization and innovation, and finally enter what

American economist Walt Rostov has termed the takeoff stage of a national economic growth.

All this is invigorating for a common man and builds respect faith and trust in political leadership. A man on the street must feel that his future is in safe hands.

The Second World War created a massive manufacturing Industry

The two world wars also gave a fillip to Industrialization of the western powers. Mobilizing the economy for Second World War finally cured the depression in the US which had had its ripple affect across major western countries too. Millions of men and women joined the armed forces, and even larger numbers went to work in well-paying defense jobs especially manufacturing. World War Two affected the world and the United States profoundly; it continues to influence us even today. War was not fought with software but with solid hardware and manpower where 15 million perished over six year's war.

Let me give some figures of hardware manufactured before and during the war for you to absorb and appreciate the scale and speed of manufacturing.

Can you believe that a total of 809,693 (more than 8 lac) aircraft were produced across all the countries including US, Russia and UK? Forty percent were produced by America! Germans produced 119,371 aircraft and America was at number one with 324,750 almost three times that of Hitler's Germany.

Russians had total Tanks and Self Propelled Guns (SPG) 131,700 in number.

US losses- 10,000 tanks/SPGs destroyed or lost.

A glimpse of other vehicles used by Americans in the war are:-

Dodge one tons 382,350 produced by US. Willey jeep WW II total: 647,925 by US. Harley Davidson Motor cycles, the largest recipient was the Soviet Union, which was sold over 30,000 Motor cycles. 572,500 Large Cargo truck 2.5 tons by US.

The political leadership in India today has enough on its hands to catchup

Modi government went for a multipronged development agenda- I would say 360 degree approach. He started work on several fronts simultaneously so that nothing is missed out- as far as possible. These have had a force multiplier effect on the economy and general wellbeing.

Every member of the team is committed to his task. The minister for transport and infrastructure Mr. Nitin Gadkari in a podcast interview quipped that John F Kennedy said 'American roads are not good because America is rich but America is rich because American Roads are good'!

The Vande Bharat Express, is an Indian semi-high-speed, intercity, train which is operated by the Indian Railways.

It was designed and manufactured by Integral Coach Factory (ICF) at, Chennai under the Indian government's Make in India initiative. The unit cost of the first rake was estimated at

₹100 crore, although it is expected to go down with subsequent production. At the original price, it is estimated to be 40% cheaper than a similar train imported from Europe. The train was launched on 15 February 2019.

Defense expo 2022

Prime Minister Narendra Modi, inaugurated the country's biggest-ever Defense Expo showcasing the products of Indian firms in Gujarat's Gandhinagar on 19 Oct 22. He said the event will strengthen the world's faith in India's business skills.

He added, "In the world, there is a monopoly of few countries. But India has made its own place now. Several countries are showing interest in Indian industries," he said.

"Over 1,300 exhibitors, including 100 start-ups, are taking part. There are foreign companies that have investments in Indian companies. In a first, over 450 MoUs and agreements are being signed," PM Modi said.

"The country will need the contribution of youth to grow in the field of space technology. This opportunity will be like a window to the future for the youth."

He claimed that in the last 5 years, the nation's defense exports have increased by 8 times.

"We are supplying defense products to over 75 countries now. Several countries are showing interest in Indian fighter jets. We are supplying defense goods to America, Israel, and many other countries. Brahmos is the best example. Brahmos is favorite among several countries."

The tide has surely turned. Better- we had turned the tide earlier.

I think the biggest strength of Prime Minister Modi is common sense and using that to take major decisions. More often than not he is spot on. His initiatives seem simple but have a profound impact across the 1.4 billion people. World over leaders can learn this and most of them hold him in very high esteem.

Late Rajiv Gandhi as the Prime Minister said that only 15 paisa out of a rupee sent by his government reached the actual beneficiary! The rest was gobbled up by the middle men. This was said in 1985 and no one found or attempted to find a solution to this seemingly complex problem and mind you Rajiv Gandhi government is rightly given the credit of computerization and automation.

All it took was common sense based vision to solve this. Remove the man from the equation! First, PM Modi under Jandhan Yojana opened bank accounts for the poorest of the poor (the most exploited by middlemen). In one shot more than 40 Crore bank accounts were opened and then the Direct Benefit Transfer (DBT) scheme implemented, literally eliminating the middle men. Along with the force multiplier effect of digital India, it hit the nail on the head. Bang.

Common sense can bring a paradigm shift and in this case it did. It was killing five birds without a stone! The poor got his entitled money, he got self-respect, the middle men got eliminated, and the poorest man sitting in the remotest corner started paying online and as a bonus larger part of economy got accounted for.

Public trust leads to greater compliance with a wide range of public policies, such as public health responses, regulations and the tax system. It also nurtures political participation, strengthens social cohesion, and builds institutional legitimacy. In the longer term, trust is needed to help governments tackle long-term societal challenges such as climate change, ageing populations, and changing labor markets.

As a techno manager I always say 'Creating a technology is one thing but using it for mass impact is more important '.

Another leak was fixed by the government by neem coating the urea which is subsidized for farmers' use at Rs 5,360 per ton, was being diverted for industrial use especially in paints and ply wood industry, as it is cheaper compared to the urea for industrial use which costed Rs 22,000-23,000 per ton.

Look at the Medal tallies in games. A push from top has helped our sportsmen and women to do better in international arena and also linked Yoga with fitness.

Common sense again came handy. We had the means all along but were always scared of a self-created mental glass ceiling. We never thought we could do it. It took a concerted effort to get going in this going North and several initiatives were taken in this direction. For instance the Statue of Unity of Sardar Patel 597 feet tall is the tallest statue in the world. It was built with a twin purpose. First to build a world's tallest statue and second give the well-deserved due to Sardar Patel our first home minister who single handedly united all states of India as one nation. The spin off was the pride which has no price, it is priceless. Again killing three birds with one stone. In comparison, Statue of Liberty located on Liberty Island in Upper New York Bay, off the coast of New York City the highly touted monument in the US stands at 305 feet only. Almost dwarfed in front of ours.

Here also the naysayers were quick to retort. 'This statue costed around INR 3000 crore, we could feed crores of people with this!' can you believe this? Back to freebees mentality.

Questions to answer

1. How does risk taking matter in building political trust?
2. Is democracy the best form of governance? Explain.
3. How WW2 helped the USA?
4. Are Faith and Trust same? Explain in your words.
5. Why building political trust is difficult?

CHAPTER 12

BUILDING FALSE TRUST

Trust dies but mistrust blossoms.
— **Sophocles**

*I*t may not be wrong to say that 'today we live in the age of deceit and cheating'. Basic reason for this is low moral values that our society has been impacted with. Greed and too much too soon, hook or by crook mindset is the reason too. As they say 'everything is fair in love and war' now it could be 'everything is fair in everything'. Today people don't care what you think of morals and values- and it is the most unfortunate thing to happen. It is across the world.

The people targeted for 'trusting' an entity can be referred to as 'trust victims'.

Some people- not all- can do anything for fame or money or even power; whatever suits you.

Therefore the general trust by humankind on humankind has taken a hit. I remember thirty or forty years ago giving lift to some stranded along the road in a car was a done thing. People didn't hesitate at all. Today things are different, people neither give lift to a woman nor a man- young or old. And there are warnings appearing on media, also social media that 'do not give lift to a stranger'. This is a strange dip in our morals collectively.

People have been robbed, girls raped, cars stolen at gun point and the con list is pretty long. The worst is that the conman or con-women is always ahead of you and the law - coming up with innovative ways to do the job. The overall society suffers and even genuine guys cannot expect help.

Building trust 'to deceive others' is the new normal.

The bottom line is to stay alert all the time and create multiple safety measures for yourself and your family.

At an individual level

False trust is built by someone deliberately to create an impression of being good and honest. It goes to leave an impact on the 'trust victim' that 'I am trustworthy so you can deal with me safely'. It is a false narrative built to mislead the 'victim'. In the most rudimentary terms it is like 'conning someone'. You first win trust of a person and then cheat him is the modus operandi.

This has become more prevalent because of hi tech gadgets and means to reach people online. It is now called 'online fraud' or cybercrime in general.

Right from a domestic help, driver and peon upwards this builds right up to political leadership- of course methods differ.

A family or a couple hire let us say a domestic help. You may go for a police verification of the person using documents submitted by that person. It is now at least recorded in public records. Since migration and movement of people is so easy it is very difficult to be hundred percent sure of the antecedents of that person.

Though the police run the details of the person through their system, it can only find if the person has past criminal record and cannot guarantee his bad or nefarious intentions. These software systems have limited data base and with all this effort, a thug may escape without being detected.

Police verification may not be foolproof but it creates a psychological impact on the applicant. At least a criminal element would not apply for police verification.

If all these systems were fool proof we would not be having any crime in the society.

There are several cases where the employer is cheated by the employee and this happens more often than not in cases where the employer is callous and has not done due diligence. Theft, robbery or even murders happen because of domestic help going astray.

In most of the countries the police system is so much overloaded with these incidents that it is difficult for the law to catch up with the criminal.

"trust, but verify," the Russian proverb made famous by former US President Ronald Reagan should be the rule of thumb to avoid regretting later.

At an organizational level

Though ethics is a favorite topic in the corporate parlance, it still has a long way to go. The root of the problem is 'going gung ho on profits'. Bottom line is that CEO's are hired and fired only on bottom lines. Many entrepreneurs have gone under as they never did due financial diligence and went overboard only to go bust. They wanted to push the bottom line up and the bottom line pushed them to the bottom.

Most suffered as they wanted too much too soon – related issue to values.

Case in point is the financial crisis of 2008. Experts felt that it was a financial exuberance/oversight but also a 'moral oversight'. In the US, the Fed Funds Rate was cut from 6.25% to 1.75% in 2001. The rate was then cut further and was held at 1% until mid-2004. There was a tide in financial markets and that the US government in particular, and regulators more generally, swam strongly with the tide and encouraged it. It is the 'moral responsibility' of the regulator to keep a check to avoid 'snowball effect'. They are paid for this and so are the bankers! You can't wash off your hands.

It began with cheap credit and 'lax (derelict) lending standards' – caution thrown to the winds as long as you meet your sales targets of giving out loans- to every Tom, Dick or Harry - that fueled a housing bubble. Un-lent funds in the American banks accumulate opportunity losses, so the outlandish lending. They are forced to lend with risks gone astray. When the bubble burst, the banks were left holding trillions of dollars of worthless investments in subprime mortgages. This financial crisis stretched over a year, causing the collapse of Lehman Brothers in September 2008. The collapse of Lehman Brothers marked the largest bankruptcy in US history. It not only impacted the US but had a ripple effect across economies. The Great Recession that followed cost many their jobs, their savings, and their homes. Investment bankers were ducking and looking for a place to hide.

With the major US stock market indexes suffering from their worst losses as the Treasury Department, White House and Congress struggled to put forward a comprehensive plan to prevent the crisis and to restore confidence (Aka trust) in the economy.

Espionage – moles

Planting moles in rival gangs is an age old trick in every book. You make your own guy convince the rival gang (especially its leader) that he or she wants to join the gang. Once he wins the trust by demonstrating his loyalty he is taken in as a trusted man on the deck. He enters basis the misplaced trust and keeps giving his previous gang important information to finally do what he was planted for.

The same happens in case of espionage where spies are either cultivated or planted carefully in the rival government machineries. They are like planting a Trojan horse. A human Trojan horse also gets all the inputs basis trust that he gradually cultivates. It is a slow but a sure and workable method. KGB and CIA as well as Mossad and MI6 had done it for decades.

At political level

Building trust at political level is also something that has been done for ages. Here you need to dupe or win the trust of millions if not billions. Every time it may not be a false narrative, especially in democracies it has to be as close to reality as possible. Sometimes it may appear that the electorate has been taken for a ride. As mentioned earlier, trust is an emotion and most people vote on emotional rather than rational thinking. A good mix of both- rational and emotional- is required in politics to win the trust of masses.

Today politicians have several tools- especially technology driven media, social or otherwise through which you can reach a man's or a woman's heart and head through their bed room screens or landing right on palm tops.

No wonder rhetoric is a part of political teaching and it works by building a perception which builds trust.

Rhetoric began as an art and a craft in Greece where students were trained to develop tactics of oratorical persuasion. Rhetoric originated in a school of pre-Socratic philosophers known as the Sophists circa 600 BC. It was also used in legal arguments- no wonder most politicians end up as law makers on the basis of rhetoric.

Rhetoric is associated with persuasion in public and political settings such as assemblies and courts of law. Because of relationship with democratic institutions, it thrives in democracies with rights of free speech, and expression.

Yet and I say yet, the leaders who demonstrate a sense of commitment earn the respect of their electorate, if you are committed your work and throughput shows. People do watch carefully and an average voter especially in developing economies who has been kept deprived for long can discern between wheat and chaff and he votes for 'wheat'. First impression can be the last impression but it may not last very long.

> 'Mistrust first impulses; they are nearly always good.'
> **– Charles Maurice de Talleyrand**

What is the way out?

There are no easy answers to this as 'values and morals' in the entire society have taken a big hit. Bench marks of success have shifted from 'great people' to 'the rich and mighty people'. This is applicable to the entire population of the world. May be tiny pockets, in areas where media has had a lesser impact have been spared. God knows for how long they will remain, grounded and preserve trust amongst them.

While writing school books on 'Values and life skills' (from grade 1 to 8) I had to cater for several chapters in almost every class book on how to protect yourself from bad elements in the society and how to keep yourself safe from people who are out to con you. Of course a lot of content is to instill 'good values' for them to become honest citizens. No point of creating global citizens who cannot be trusted or are dishonest.

Value education has taken a back seat in our education system as there is a race for getting better grades in subjects that matter. These are the ones which get you a better college, and better jobs. Parents have a very big role to play as a child spends larger portion of a 24 hour day at home. Parents have two or three kids to handle whereas the school teachers have a much larger number of students to handle!

I feel parents and powers that be must insist on teaching and practicing good moral values in schools if we need to see and experience any change. The society has to 'boot strap' itself out of the mess we have ourselves created.

Making and framing more laws and rules cannot be the answer to 'false' trust' when the society itself is downright corrupt and cares little for morals and honesty.

Value education I insist is like 'climate change'; everyone is talking about it- it is staring you in your face and now hitting you hard too- but no one is doing anything about it.

Counter measures

Electronic Warfare analogy can again be used to demonstrate the way to counter 'fake or false trust' building exercise by the 'trust victim'. You have ECM (Electronic Counter Measures) which is an electrical or electronic device designed to trick or deceive radar, sonar, or other detection systems.

And to counter that you have ECCM, is a part of electronic warfare which includes a variety of practices which attempt to reduce or eliminate the effect of electronic countermeasures (ECM) on electronic sensors aboard vehicles, ships and aircraft and weapons such as missiles. ECCM is also known as electronic protective measures (EPM).

At an individual level if you are being fed 'false trust signals' you need to create a counter protective measure for yourself. There is no one window solution for this. Today not only technology but the crooks are becoming smarter too. They are generally ahead of the law and also in the learning curve. You need to remain alert all the time. If you are aware that there is a danger or you are getting duped then err on the cautious side. Don't feel embarrassed to check and countercheck facts and antecedents whatever it takes. It does take extra time and builds stress but there is little choice we have. As they say 'it is too good to be true' use this axiom. Whenever in doubt.

Unfortunately this leads to further mistrust in the society.

'I sweat. If anything comes easy to me I mistrust it.'
– Lilli Palmer

Questions to answer

1. What is the basic reason for so much mistrust today in the society?
2. Do you feel good value system can create better trusting society? Illustrate with example.
3. What kind of due diligence you will carry out hiring a driver at home?
4. How do you build trust within your family? Do you trust each member blindly?
5. How do you vote? Do you deliberately evaluate the intentions and work of the government, or you go by your gut feeling?

CHAPTER 13

PEOPLE YOU CAN TRUST

'Human nature is not black and white but black and grey'
– Graham Greene

Having read this book where I have covered different aspects of trust in different settings, you would now be clued up on the basic idea and importance of this highly prized characteristic for everything that matters.

Being trust worthy is an important and valued trait for every one of us. Some people are trusted and some are not. This trait of being dependable, reliable and loyal is a sterling quality of any person.

If your friends, family and colleagues and bosses feel you can be relied upon, it is a great feeling.

It is important to keep a watch on people you deal with every day- especially on the 'Trust part'.

In this chapter I am going to touch a touchy subject of 'personal trust'- that too on the basis of sun signs! Many people don't believe in Sun signs and many do. No wonder every magazine, news portal, paper carries 'This week for you' kind of a half pager and it is like a forecast of the week. Unless people were reading it for whatever its worth, why would they publish it?

Having said that I believe that you cannot forecast in twelve buckets (12 Zodiac Signs) the future of 8 billion people of this planet. But one thing is evident that people born under different Zodiac signs behave differently and those in the same bucket do have certain personal traits pretty similar and pronounced.

Sun signs divides the earths close to eight billion population into 12 distinct zodiac signs. These are considered the 12 basic personality types. People in these groups get their characteristics or personality traits from whatever sign that the sun was passing through at the time of their birth.

Sun signs define the character and personalities for people born under different sun signs. Here also, the characteristics are loosely defined and loosely structured. It is more of a narrative rather than a grading (numerical) system. These are mere approximations and indicators only. I feel one needs to leave it at that. If these can give us a gross feel about our basic character, we can take that as a starting point for deeper interpretation.

Surprisingly, these characteristics pretty well match up with things like our sense of humor, delayed gratification, creativity, perseverance, optimism, patience, trusting others, impulsive nature, caring for others, and so on.

They also talk of dependability and loyalty as a human characteristic. A lot many people have done research basis zodiac signs, I am only extrapolating the existing content and trying to establish only one point that human nature is a natural gift and people have strong traits according to their zodiac sign. This should not be taken as a gospel truth but only as an indicator of human character to be so much predictable yet not written, engraved on stone- with a pinch of salt.

In this chapter I would discuss very briefly, only three sun signs that are top ranked as 'trustworthy' people. This again can change as other experts in this area may have difference of opinion. Be as it may, let me give a brief idea of top three sun signs. Though science has rejected astrology as a meaningful science, there are several experts who regularly write about this- and people read them.

For instance Mary Alice Kemery, popularly known as Linda Goodman was a New York Times bestselling American astrologer and poet. She wrote the first astrology book to make the New York Times Best Seller list. People do have faith and faith has no reasons.

> *"Astrology reveals the will of the gods."*
>
> **– Juvenal**

Trustworthiness, can be seen in different ways. To gauge the loyalty or trust quotient of different sun signs, you need to consider a few aspects of human behavior. Can a person keep a secret, comes to mind first? Will the person come to you for call immediately if you want him or her?

Will such people be always truthful to you? Will you trust him to finish an assignment on time? Humans are very complex especially when it comes to behavior in different settings. Someone may be trustworthy in one way…and not so much in something else. He may behave when things are good but may let you down under pressure!

According to many surveys which rank TQ basis sun signs -The first or on top of the stack is Virgo.

VIRGO (August 23 – September 22)

Virgo is supposed to be the epitome of trustworthiness and is honest and reliable. They are punctual, thorough and go into details. "They're very truthful and apply their minds to any problem that comes on their table." A Virgo is always going to tell you the truth which could sometime be a little harsh, but they're really well meaning.

'Hard work is a good way of winning hearts' is their philosophy. They seldom display emotions and not easily express love as it is usually done. Therefore you can trust them with work without expecting much emotional response.

Their boss will always be happy with their performance, which they carry out perfectly. They are organized and their desk is usually pretty neat and clean. They do create good work ethics around themselves- home or office.

Virgos are generous to others who are genuinely in need. They let their heart rule their head. Virgos are happiest when they are solving problems for others.

Some well-known Virgos are

Sophia Loren, Leo Tolstoy, Lyndon Johnson, PM Narendra Modi

The second most trustworthy sun sign is Taurus.

TAURUS (April 20 to May 20)

Bull is the sign of Taurus. It will not be wrong to sum up this personality as "Rock of a relationship or a friendship."

They are not the kind of people who will take the easier path, in fact, they would take the more difficult route to achieve their ambition rather than taking shortcuts. For a Taurian everything is backed by hard work. They are not overambitious and are pretty content by nature. That is why no 'cut throat' attitude for them.

Loyalty to family, colleagues and friends is their second nature. They are a likeable and therefore, people respect them and are fond of them. Impartial by nature, revenge does not form a part of their nature. They are generous and do reach out to people whenever they need them. Very dependable people with a high degree of self-respect.

They believe in fair play, and people consider them to be trustworthy. Because you are dependable and reliable, people respect you and come forward to seek your help.

Some famous ones are:- Sachin Tendulkar, Harry S Truman, Andre Agassi and Al Pacino

AQUARIAN (January 20 - February 18)

They are to a large extent intellectuals and artistic and people come to them to seek guidance on originality and creativity.

They are cause-oriented, patriotic and tend to do things that are good for the society or humanity. Sensitive to other's needs they, display a good amount of empathy. Very gentle and, humanitarian, and many times over-permissive.

They believe in 'Charity begins at home' and are philanthropic by nature.' And therefore 'Doing good for others' is in their blood.

Aquarians are prepared to listen to the other side of the story. Very principled, honest and loyal to coworker's, friends and the organization they work for.

They display moral courage and often stand up for others, which sometimes can be troublesome. They are not diplomatic, many times being tactless and rude and that is what people don't like in them. But they are well meaning. Being 'fair to all' attitude makes them a good boss and also a good colleague. Not being partial, is taken as their strength by friends, bosses, and even their subordinates. They tend to trust others, and many a time can be taken for a ride for this reason.

To display courage and to protect those who have been wronged makes them trustworthy. Seen as a 'well meaning' person, they are respected by others.

Some famous ones are:-

Abraham Lincoln, Oprah Winfrey, General Douglas MacArthur, Mozart and Franklin D Roosevelt

Aquarius; *Wants to tell you a story, but with 27 tangents and an 83 percent chance that they'll forget where they were going with it. But it was worth it!*

Questions to answer

1. Do you believe in Zodiac signs?
2. Do you feel Astrology has some meaning?
3. Have you noticed similar traits in same sun signs of friends and family?
4. Name five famous people other than given in the chapter who have a sun sign of Aquarius.

EPILOGUE

Trust Intelligence

Sharpen your trust axe every day

"Intelligence is the ability to adapt to change."
— **Stephen Hawking**

Having gone through relevance of this enigmatic human quality in different scenarios and settings, described in detail in this book, by now you would be convinced that it is a human trait, competence or ability which lets you navigate and glide through anything that you set your eyes on. With this under your belt, you can win hearts and also make people follow you.

It also has a connect with your sun sign, like your emotional responses in general.

It ought to be some kind of competence or intelligence which helps us work on a day to day dealings with people and public at large. Some people have inborn quality of radiating or ability to divaricate positive vibes and many need to learn to acquire this - much like charisma.

Epilogue

Though there is no one single acceptable definition of 'intelligence' which has been discussed over century's right from the time of Socrates and Aristotle.

Socrates said "Intelligent individuals learn from everything and everyone; average people, from their experiences. The stupid already have all the answers."

I like the simplest definition of intelligence given as under.

'Intelligence is the ability to think, **to learn from experience***, to solve problems, and* **to adapt to new situations. Intelligence is important because it has an impact on many human behaviors.***'*

The ones which are of interest to me in this context are

Experiential learning, adapting and its impact on a human behavior at multiple levels.

If you make efforts to improve your linguistic skills you can do that with hard work, practice and conscious efforts. Similarly you – if you so decide- can work on building trust. These are 'confidence building measures' or simply building bridges to reach out to others and make them like you and allow them to rely on you and respect you.

Let me reiterate that even if you can take your trustworthiness northwards by 20% it will make you feel desirable, acceptable and at peace with yourself. Life will become really worth living in every sense of the word.

So go for it. Remember you need to sharpen your 'trust axe' regularly, consciously and if possible every day.

"The measure of intelligence is the ability to change."
— **Albert Einstein**

www.ingramcontent.com/pod-product-compliance
Lightning Source LLC
LaVergne TN
LVHW041711070526
838199LV00045B/1300